Mexicano communities are some of the oldest, most widespread immigrant communities in the history of the United States. Their resilient nature and their increasing number create an important contemporary case for understanding the relationship between language socialization and bilingualism. The description of Eastside, a Mexicano community in northern California, provides a window into the rich and complex sociolinguistic milieu of such communities.

Pushing Boundaries is a fascinating account that considers language learning and socialization in the context of real, problematic, and important activities in people's lives. The authors describe ways in which bilingual children and their families actively and innovatively use the linguistic and cultural resources available to them. We learn that Mexicano parents are responsible and deliberate participants in their children's language socialization; that bilingual school-age children rely on knowledge sources that extend well beyond their immediate neighborhoods; and that children using their skills as cultural and linguistic brokers are an invaluable resource for their families.

Educators, psychologists, public policy advocates, as well as scholars of sociolinguistics and urban studies will find the descriptions of the bilingual child of Eastside insightful and useful.

Pushing Boundaries

Pushing Boundaries
Language and Culture in a Mexicano Community

OLGA A. VASQUEZ
UNIVERSITY OF CALIFORNIA, SAN DIEGO

LUCINDA PEASE-ALVAREZ
UNIVERSITY OF CALIFORNIA, SANTA CRUZ

SHEILA M. SHANNON
UNIVERSITY OF COLORADO, DENVER

CAMBRIDGE
UNIVERSITY PRESS

Published by the Press Syndicate of the University of Cambridge
The Pitt Building, Trumpington Street, Cambridge CB2 1RP
40 West 20th Street, New York, NY 10011-4211, USA
10 Stamford Road, Oakleigh, Melbourne 3166, Australia

First published 1994

Printed in the United States of America

Library of Congress Cataloging-in-Publication Data

Vasquez, Olga A.
Pushing boundaries : language and culture in a Mexicano community
/ Olga A. Vasquez, Lucinda Pease-Alvarez, Sheila M. Shannon.
p. cm.
Includes bibliographical references and index.
ISBN 0-521-41935-2
1. Sociolinguistics – California. 2. Mexicans – California –
Languages. 3. Language and culture – California. I. Pease-
Alvarez, Lucinda. II. Shannon, Sheila M. III. Title.
P40.45.U5V37 1994
306.4'4'09794–dc20 93-38810
CIP

A catalog record for this book is available from the British Library

ISBN 0-521-41935-2 hardback

Para los niños cuyas voces cantan la verdad
y
muy especialmente a Laura, Pilar, Rigel, y Tom
whose understanding helped us along.

Contents

Foreword

A few weeks before reading this book, I visited my good friend and colleague Pedro Pedraza in New York City, actually in East Harlem, well known as Spanish Harlem, or "El Barrio." Pedro, a sociolinguist, had mentioned the possibility of developing an ethnographic study of Mexicans in East Harlem. That's right, Mexicans. In the last four years or so he had noticed an appreciable number of Mexicans in what is predominantly a Puerto Rican, and, more recently, a Dominican community. One could spot young Mexican families, parents and children, walking in the neighborhood, street-corner vendors selling what one could identify as Mexican wares, and Mexican men and women working in the local shops. A teacher in a nearby school had told Pedro that she had received some new students from Mexico, mostly from Puebla, in central Mexico, and there were now *bodegas* where one could purchase Mexican products and eat Mexican food with a distinctive *estilo* from Puebla, and we noticed that these places were becoming the primary centers of interaction for the newcomers. In short, all the signs were there indicating the rapid incorporation of a new ethnic group into El Barrio. But why? Why East Harlem in New York City? And how are these immigrants making out in these difficult circumstances? How are they learning English? What are the children experiencing in school?

As we toured the neighborhood, Pedro pointed out a Mexican adolescent boy hanging out on a street corner. From his attire, pose, mannerisms, and the music he was listening to, he appeared to be just another kid in El Barrio. "He's been here for a while now," Pedro said chuckling, "and check him out: he looks part

Puerto Rican, part Dominican, and part Black, but he's a Mexican kid." He looked so unlike Chicano adolescents in, say, East Los Angeles, or Mexican kids in South Tucson, for that matter. But why shouldn't he? Not only is he growing up under very different social, historical, and cultural circumstances but, as this book explains, in order to survive he is making use of qualitatively different "intercultural transactions," creating meaning from the language, knowledge, and resources available to him from the home, the community, and the school. But, is he still Mexican? Yes, I would argue, he is as Mexicano as the children and families who make up the community of "Eastside," whom we meet in this book. However, he is as different from these children as El Barrio is from Eastside.

This volume offers important insights into how people, adults and children, in various circumstances of life, actively and innovatively use the cultural resources afforded by their experiences and their social relationships in pursuit of their goals. The authors, each of whom independently conducted studies within the same community in northern California, invite us to take an intimate glimpse at life, not as some sort of sociological abstraction, but at the social transactions, the face-to-face encounters, that constitute life for people within this Mexicano neighborhood in California. In these pages we witness field trips with adolescent students, examine family conversations about problems in living, visit a doctor with a mother and her daughter (as translator), and go to school with preschoolers to listen in on their conversations with adults, among other events that come from the researchers' direct experience (and recording) of the phenomena they were trying to study. These three colleagues were there, in situ, for many months, and their chapters transport us there as well, to observe, to interact, and to understand with them as they interpret what they see and hear.

But these events are not just presented as mere descriptions; the authors rely primarily on the presentation of transcripts, the participants' own discourses, that are then interpreted contextually and theoretically. The people studied are not presented as stereotypes but as they are, all different from each other – all active, dynamic, and diverse human beings making intelligent uses of their social, cultural, and linguistic resources to live and to learn. Readers should also be ready for some challenges and controversies: First, there is the strong proposal that "literate" thinking, usually associated with the intentional manipulation or analysis of texts, especially in school settings, has an oral base that is documentable in family conversations. In brief, the claim is that we have seriously underestimated, especially with working-class and "minority" families, the nature and quality of oral interactions, while privileging (middle-class) print-based interactions in developing literate uses of language.

There is also the claim that considerable convergence exists between language interaction patterns in this community and those patterns reported by other researchers working with middle-class Anglo children, leading the authors to label as untenable the argument that home-school discontinuities can predict either school success or failure for an entire cultural group. But surely the discontinuities hypothesis is but one aspect of a broader argument, which also highlights the nature of the schooling experience itself, the social interactions that constitute classroom life and define students as successes or failures. And indeed, these classroom interactions also appear central in implementing the authors' recommendations that teachers, as a fundamental aspect of their pedagogy, take full advantage of students' and families' resources for learning, their language and cultural experiences, in developing advanced environments for learning in school.

I am very grateful that my three colleagues invited me to write this foreword to their fine volume. It is an important book, with much to offer, whether one is interested in children and families in the east side of Lincoln City, California, or in East Harlem, New York City.

Luis C. Moll
University of Arizona

Preface

Everyone faces boundaries as they go about their daily living. Some are formidable, some flexible, and many more are imperceptible. Regardless of our ethnicity, gender, or social class, we all participate in a multiplicity of worlds of the home, family, workplace, and an array of secondary institutions. Sometimes, traveling from one world to another is unconscious and effortless. At other times, crossing a boundary separating realms of activity and behavior may be a little more than stepping across a line. In fact, the mere existence of a boundary as a marker of a physical or conceptual expanse of the universe – with its own space, knowledge, language, or behavior – however, does not guarantee its impenetrability. People, material goods, and modes of thought always seem to find a way to get to the other side of boundaries intent on barring exchange. In fact, more often than not, we routinely push boundaries to the limits of their elasticity. We try a new look, we venture out of familiar surroundings, and on occasion we shed old ways of thinking for new ones that fit more appropriately to our existing reality.

Reflecting over the time the three of us spent interacting with the Mexicano community of Eastside, we found that this was definitely the case in our own personal journeys. The metaphor of language "pushing boundaries" came from noting that as individuals, we pushed the many boundaries that encapsulated us as teachers, students, researchers, partners, mothers, interpreters, and ethnic group members. Although we faced lines of class, educational background, and knowledge of language and culture from a position of privilege, we found ourselves trying new foods and experimenting with new roles vis-à-vis our families and loved ones. Our children even accompanied us in much of our research activities. And, our own teaching and learning began to reflect the collaborative nature of activities that we encountered in the homes and the community. Our experiences in the east side of Lincoln City, at the same time that we attended one of the most prestigious universities in the country, gave us a fuller view of our existence and of our role as educators, social scientists, and all around human beings. More importantly, it taught us that the perfect location in which to conduct our work was within these boundaries. Thus, the dichotomies between the home, school, community, and mainstream institutions were not as clear-cut as conventional wisdom would have it. Like language, we found ourselves constantly moving in and out of insider-outsider roles and vice versa.

Although there is much to share about our own personal experiences and our development as scholars through our work with the community of Eastside, this book highlights the insights we gained from consolidating three separate ethnographic studies that spanned a period of six years in the Mexican immigrant community of Lincoln City. We each spent a year or more in various activities in the community before spending approximately two years conducting our separate studies: Pease-Alvarez volunteered in a children's preschool, Vásquez worked as a research assistant in a school-based university project, and Shannon studied how language was used in a bilingual class in one of the local elementary schools. Because of our involvement in the local schools prior to our studies, we each entered the homes of Eastsiders as *maestras* [teachers], a label we tried hard to cast aside. Our fluency in Spanish, our many experiences living in other ethnic communities as well as being mothers of elementary-school-age children helped us achieve, instead, the role of friend and/or group member.

Although the similarities among the three studies helped us to consolidate the findings into one view of language learning and socialization in a Mexican immigrant community, it was not an easy task to integrate our research. In fact, it took over a year of working through issues of analysis and interpretation before we reached consensus on the view we advance here. Through intensive deliberations we were able to interweave interactions that portray how the daily activities of Mexicanos of Eastside play a part in language learning and socialization practices. We demonstrate the circumstances in which the second language and culture enters the home, how immigrant individuals learn to draw from multiple knowledge sources to meet the challenges of daily life, and finally, through examples of educational activities, how our particular view of language and culture can be applied to teaching and learning.

Along the way, many people assisted and contributed to our work. We would like to thank all those individuals of Eastside who opened their homes and their daily lives to our inspection. We chose to maintain their anonymity but their identities will always be remembered in our hearts. We specially would like to thank Antonio Alvarez (affectionately known as Toño) for his patience and his holding down the fort with two extra children while we worked into the night. Our children, Laura, Pilar, Rigel and Tom, we thank for their understanding and their support through the length of the project. For their thoughtful comments on the many versions of our work, we thank Michael Cole, Bud Mehan, Luis Moll, Kenji Hakuta, Roberto Calderón, Nancy Commins, René Galindo, and the collaborators at the Laboratory of Comparative Human Cognition at the University of California, San Diego, who dedicated several lab sessions to versions of our chapters. Rosalina Calderón's comments on the nuances of our interpretations are also much appreciated. We are also grateful for the assistance of Kathy Mooney, Tricia Henry, and Yolanda Pacheco James in the preparation of the manuscript. We would also like to thank the UCSD Chancellor's Fellowship that provided the resources for Vásquez to coordinate the development of this book project as a post-doctoral fellow. Finally, we thank Tom Shannon for creating the maps of Eastside.

Chapter 1

Introduction

Everyday uses of language influence what we do, think, and learn. The conversations that we have on issues that concern us contribute to the formation of our opinions and theories. The talk that accompanies the solution of a problem or the completion of an unfamiliar task contributes to learning how to approach similar problems and tasks. The talk that involves our children contributes to their learning of language and ways of the society into which they are born. Thus, the language we use is a tool that mediates our thinking and learning. Moreover, it is an important window into the social and intellectual worlds of its users.

In this book we capitalize on this revelatory function of language to provide a window into the intellectual and social, or, to be more specific, cultural resources of individuals who are members of a Mexican immigrant community we call Eastside. Our descriptions of the language that involves children in this community yields a positive and dynamic portrayal of their socialization experiences. Through our careful examinations of their talk, we have learned that adults and children who live in this community deliberately seek out and draw upon a range of linguistic and cultural resources to meet the challenges of a complex, unfamiliar and, sometimes, oppressive society.

At the heart of our work lies a concern with the interrelationships that exist between language, culture, learning, and knowledge. Because these domains interact, information about one also yields important insights about another. This is perhaps most obvious when considering the case of cultural anthropologists who spend a considerable amount of time learning the language and sociolinguistic norms of the members of a particular culture as a prelude to understanding their beliefs, values, behaviors, and social relationships. To be truly proficient in the language, however, anthropologists must acquire more than the ability to communicate. They must also acquire the ability to "interpret people's feelings and attitudes in actual speech situations" (Paredes, 1984, p. 3). Relying on dictionary definitions may prove misleading. For example, Paredes describes an occasion when an anthropologist studying political behavior in a Chicano community missed the meaning of a conversation when he relied on the standard dictionary definition of the Anglicism *movida*. Interpreting the conversation within the framework of a common stereotype of Chicanos in the 1960s as a "sleeping giant," the anthropologist mistook the word *movida* to mean agitate. Paredes' more accurate cultural definition of the term is contained in the following passage.[1]

> . . . Chicanos long ago substituted *movida* (apparently a direct translation of the English noun "move") for *jugada*, in the sense of a maneuver or move in a game of strategy. The term usually has negative connotations: *movida chueca* (crooked maneuver); *hay mucha movida* (there's dirty work going on); *hacer movida* (to look out for number one) (emphasis in original, p.4).

This aspect of language proficiency, known as communicative competence, allows individuals in everyday situations to communicate in culturally appropriate ways across a variety of situations. It is communicative competence that makes it possible for interpreting the underlying social relationships and norms of interactions. It influences which language variety is used, how it is used, and the purpose for which it is used. According to this socially and culturally defined view of language, individuals draw upon their knowledge of culture as they create the meaning of speech and its extralinguistic features, such as tone, gestures, and social context. They rely on cultural information to interpret social convention, idiomatic usage, and style (Hymes, 1972). The speaker and hearer are not only conversational partners but are interpreters of culture as well. Without this competency, individuals, like Paredes' anthropologist, commit serious errors about the meanings implicit in a group's language and culture (e.g., "seeing Chicanos as passive, apolitical, and incapable of organizing much of anything [p.4]," when indeed, the conversation was politically motivated).

Culture, along with other social variables, contributes to the variations that exist in the way we express ourselves through language. This is particularly evident in within-language variation, where even individuals from the same language background may interpret and use language differently, according to the norms of their particular community. For example, on a trip to Spain, Vásquez inadvertently asked the hotel clerk to examine her physically when she used, *"Me quiero registrar"* to mean "I would like to check in." The clerk, seizing an opportunity to establish a status differential, curtly informed her that *registrar* meant "inspect" or "search" in *Castellano* [Castilian Spanish] and that she should have said, *"Me quiero inscribir."* This brief interaction communicates much about the social and cultural assumptions underlying the use of language. One could speculate on the influence that Vásquez's physical appearance, her Chicano cadence, and/or her gender may have had on the clerk's response, but there is little doubt that, at least in his own estimation, the clerk's command of standard Spanish afforded him a higher status and the right to correct a guest's use of language.

It is important to underscore that differences in language use arise out of varying cultural contexts and, as Hymes

3

(1972) has argued need not, "be a bar to full command of the cognitive possibilities of language" (p. xxxi). Variations in the language children learn to use and the way they use it reflects differences in their groups' cultural practices and perspectives. Yet, the fact that some children do not learn to master certain uses of language in the context of their homes and communities does not mean that they cannot be consciously developed in other contexts. In short, we have known for some time that language variation does not imply a cognitive deficit. Yet, the language experiences of children from ethnolinguistic groups continue to be misunderstood and discounted as inappropriate in ways reminiscent of the experience that involved Vásquez and the hotel clerk.

Schooling is one context where the language experiences of diverse learners are consistently misunderstood, ignored, or intentionally reshaped to fit a specified cultural form (Mehan, 1991). Instead of organizing instruction in ways that add to and extend the abilities of children from diverse groups, many teachers and administrators rely on interactional patterns that dismiss linguistic and cultural variation as inappropriate and deficient. Ways of speaking such as "known-answer questions, uses of ideas out of context, and grouping ideas into abstract taxonomies and schemas" (p.4) which often appear counterintuitive to some groups (Scribner and Cole, 1981; Heath, 1983) dominate instructional interaction in the classroom to the exclusion of others. Moreover, ethnic minority children who are not native speakers of Standard English tend to be enrolled in classrooms where instruction emphasizes rote and lock-step approaches to the acquisition of basic skills and English. Consequently, many, if not most, of these students never gain access to the more enriched, integrated, and cognitively demanding curriculum typically available to students who are white and middle or upper class. It is not surprising, then, that so few Mexicano/Latino,[2] African American, and Native American students never gain access to the academic experiences necessary for admittance into colleges and universities.[3]

Introduction

CROSS-CULTURAL VARIATION IN LANGUAGE SOCIALIZATION

The relationship between language and culture has important implications for the socialization of children. Through their participation in the language milieu that is part of their everyday lives, children learn the beliefs, values, and ways of the group into which they are born, as well as its linguistic code. Thus, the language that surrounds and involves children plays a critical role in their overall development. It is the means through which they are socialized and enculturated as well as the raw data they draw upon for acquiring language. As Heath so succinctly put it, "language learning is cultural learning" (1986, p. 145).

A number of factors that vary across cultures have been identified as sources of differences in language socialization experiences of children from different backgrounds. Studies by Ochs (1988), Schieffelin and Ochs (1986), and Heath (1983) indicate that culturally specific views on child raising and language learning influence the ways parents and other adults interact verbally with children. The role and status of children in the society is directly related to the way adults converse with them. Middle-class Anglo parents who believe that language learning is facilitated by adapting the situation to their child tend to assist their children's language learning endeavors by engaging them in conversations and by accommodating their own talk in a variety of ways. For example, they choose certain topics and talk about them in ways that they feel take into account their child's ability and interests. They often use a simplified, repetitive, and affect-laden register known as "baby talk" or "motherese." They elicit clarifications and elaborations, expand and extend children's utterances, and regularly engage children in predictable conversational routines. Heath (1983) provides an example of how adults in an Anglo community seize upon a child's utterances to expand and interpret her speech:

5

Sally, banging on the backdoor, screamed "Go kool," and Aunt Sue responded "No, Sally, you can't go to *school* yet, Lisa will be back, come on, help mamma put the pans away." Aunt Sue assumed Sally both wanted to *go to school* and was commenting on the fact that Lisa had just *gone to school*. (p. 124, emphasis in original)

These patterns of interpretive and interventionist verbal behavior have not been observed in some nonwestern and working-class communities where parents believe that children learn best by adapting to their surroundings. According to Heath, Ochs, and Schieffelin, adults in these societies do not view young children as suitable or competent conversational partners. Instead, they expect children to seek out their own opportunities to learn language by listening to and observing others. Models may be provided or cues used to help direct a child's attention, but attempts to scaffold children's verbal contributions within the context of a conversation are not part of these groups' language socialization experiences. For example, in the African American community of Trackton that Heath (1983) studied, it is the children who repeat after the adults, using the ends of adult utterances as practice. In the midst of "their noisy multi-channeled communicative environments" children in Trackton are expected to be aware of what is happening around them and are not tutored or tested on discrete elements of their surroundings. As silent observers, children are expected to become information-knowers rather than information-givers and are actively discouraged from giving information to strangers.

As the descriptions and analyses in the following chapters will make clear, in a Mexicano community, differences in language-use patterns are not always as clear-cut as research among other ethnolinguistic minorities would suggest (John, 1972; Jordan, 1977, 1984; Au, 1980; Erickson and Mohatt, 1982; Heath, 1982, 1983; Philips, 1983; Jordan and Tharp, 1984; Michaels and Collins 1984). In fact, our research provides evidence of linguistic and cultural flexibility and adaptability in the use and learning of language. At times, community members use language in ways that are reminiscent of patterns found in schools and middle-class homes; other times their uses of language clearly reflect their Mexican heritage (e.g., their use of folklore, rhymes, riddles). Finally, there are occasions when the immigrant experience necessitates the development and use of unique speech patterns (Guerra, 1991). Chicano and Mexicano youth living in Mexicano communities in other parts of the country sometimes respond to the challenges of living in two cultures by developing alternative modes of oral and written expression (Cintron, 1991). For example, the oral and written language used by members of Chicano youth culture evolves by freely combining English and Spanish to form a new hybrid language. In sum, the language experience of Mexican immigrants is a complex phenomenon that defies a characterization based on simple comparisons.

LANGUAGE, CULTURE, AND SCHOOLING

For more than 30 years, researchers interested in the academic performances and circumstances of children from diverse groups have focused on the connections that exist between the social context and the use and development of language. Much of this work has examined the relationships between language, culture, and learning in areas of literacy acquisition, language development, and academic achievement. Underlying these efforts has been the concern that culture is somehow implicated in the high incidence of school failure among some groups. Several provocative, and often controversial, theories about the relationship between culturally prescribed ways of using language and failure to do well in school have generated considerable public debate. Perhaps the most insidious and enduring of these theories is one that views the background of children from diverse groups as deficient. Although, theoretically and methodologically refuted for over two decades (Cole and Bruner,

1971) the "deficit hypothesis" continues to enjoy wide application. One recent manifestation describes linguistic minority children as coming from alingual environments which lead to the development of no language or of a variety that is inferior to that used by middle class white children.

In the late 1970s the premise that failure in school can be explained by "some deficiency in these minority children and their respective cultures," shifted to one that emphasized the role of differences between learning environments (Laosa, 1977, p. 21). The cultural discontinuity perspective holds that it is not so much that children from minority homes do not have a full range of interactional competencies with which to succeed in school, but rather that their communication styles are incompatible with those of their teachers. These cultural discontinuities foster misunderstandings in teacher-student relations that lead to disciplinary problems, disruptions in the learning process, and unequal access to resources. The implications, although not often explicitly stated, are that these cultural differences prevent linguistically diverse students from acquiring the skills necessary for successful academic progress.

In this scenario, no one bears the burden of blame. The communication breakdown is seen as an "inadvertent misunderstanding – teachers and students playing into each other's cultural blind spots" (Erickson, 1987, p. 336). The "problem" lies in the different ways that groups interact, ask questions, and tell stories. Indeed, the argument presumes that if students were to come to the classroom prepared with the appropriate participation structures, questioning styles, and narrative episodes, they would succeed in school. The underlying assumption is that the master patterns for success in school that are evident in middle-class homes are not part of the socialization practices in minority homes.

An obvious solution, of course, would be to make the communicative competencies of minority children and their families more like those of the school. In actual programs developed on the basis of the difference perspective, this goal was to be accomplished at two levels. The schools were directed to institute a "culturally responsive curriculum" (Au and Mason, 1986; Erickson, 1987) that sought to incorporate minority children's communication styles into specific school teaching and learning strategies (Au and Jordan, 1981; Heath, 1982; Vogt, Jordan, and Tharp, 1987). To reach whole families, parent programs were designed to train families in those literacy-related interactions considered integral to the instructional setting (Heath, 1982; Edwards, 1987). In both the school- and home-based programs, the cultural and linguistic experiences of the children and their families were shaped to fit those of the mainstream culture.

Because the instructional objectives were to instill in the learners the discourse styles and literacy practices found in schools, the home culture was viewed as a physical context rather than as an integral part of the learning context. That is, the participants' individual contributions, including their background knowledge, skills, and general approach to reading were not generated within the context of the learning setting (Hornberger, 1989). Instead teachers incorporated certain assumed cultural characteristics of their learners into their lessons prior to the instructional activity. Thus, the curricular response to cultural differences trickles down through the teacher and does not embrace the multiple perspectives that actually exist within the classroom. In practice, it is still the child who must adapt to the pedagogy rather than the pedagogy to the child.

Overall, the strength of the discontinuity perspective lies in the empirical viability of the observed cultural and linguistic differences. Salient differences in socialization practices across cultures are well documented. However, this same strength is also the theory's chief weakness. The emphasis on differences results in an overshadowing of other factors that influence the learning setting, including school climate, teaching styles, and individual learning rates. We argue that positioning minority group socialization practices in direct opposition to those of the middle-class home and the school draws attention away from accurate descriptions of those practices and from a consideration of the possibility that other sets of relationships may exist between cultures that operate in close proximity to one another, including accommodation and biculturation. Rather than recognizing multiple perspectives and identities, proponents of the discontinuity view assume that children are forced to choose the school code over the home code. Instances of cultural similarities in communication and occasions in which children adopt neither culture's communication styles but instead develop a new style are overlooked or are dismissed as aberrations. Consideration of occasions when individuals pool knowledge and linguistic resources from the many contexts in which they participate – whether these involve mainstream culture or home culture – is also precluded by the basic assumptions of the discontinuity perspective.

As educators and social scientists, we acknowledge the discontinuities between the language and culture of the school, home, and community. However, as the work of Ogbu (1978, 1982, 1987) and others (Ogbu and Matute-Bianchi, 1986; Gibson, 1987; Suárez-Orozco, 1987; Achor and Morales, 1990; Foley, 1991) has shown, the connections between structural factors, culture, language, and learning in the school setting are much more complex and multidimensional than the discontinuity perspective espouses. Factors such as class and ideological structures, advanced by social theorists like Willis (1977), Bowles and Gintis (1976), and Bourdieu and Passeron (1990) are heavily implicated in minority school failure. That is, schooling is organized both implicitly and explicitly to promote and sustain the perspectives and institutions of those in power. Schools engage in a number of practices that favor the status quos. Middle- and upper-class English-speaking students have access to a curriculum that ultimately allows them to progress through the educational pipeline. Low-income ethnic minority students are less likely to participate in a college preparatory curriculum and more likely to drop out in significant numbers.

Erickson (1987) and Mehan (1992) argue that language differences among the many groups that participate in schools are tied to these larger societal factors. For example, Mehan

(1991) states that class along with cultural distinctions are played out in the sociolinguistics of schooling. As he puts it,

> The cultural capital of different status groups is related differently to the culture of the school. The language and socialization practices employed at home by middle- and upper-class families are reinforced by the discourse and social organization of classrooms, whereas the language and socialization practices of low-income and linguistic minority families do not match those found in the classroom. (p. 8)

Thus, Mehan reasons that discontinuities between homes and schools are tied to inequities in social structure. Schools reinforce and reward those who possess the cultural capital, including the language use practices, of the upper and middle classes.

RECONCEPTUALIZATION OF DIFFERENCE: THE RECOGNITION PERSPECTIVE

Our work, drawing upon three independently conceived and conducted ethnographic studies in one Mexicano community, has provided us with the empirical grounding to build upon existing theoretical perspectives about language, culture, and schooling. The result has been the formulation of the "recognition perspective," a view that goes beyond the simple comparative stance implicit in the discontinuity perspective to capture the similarities in language use across various contexts, the convergence of multiple knowledge sources in a single context, and the uniqueness of language use practices fostered by Mexican culture. This perspective has led us to a new conceptualization of language that frames the observation of an interaction within a context of what is there, rather than what is not. Thus, the interaction is framed within a sociocultural context that draws upon multiple histories, cultures, and languages. In this way we are able to consider the dynamic interaction of exchange between two or more cultures rather than focusing on two opposing, mutually exclusive systems. The recognition perspective allows us to replace the portrayal of an immigrant culture as one isolated from its historical and contemporary surroundings with a new vision of a vital culture, rich in linguistic inheritance, full of positive and creative possibilities that maintain and at the same time enhance both the home and school cultures and languages. We find that Mexicano culture in the United States exists within an intersection of multiple cultures and languages rather than isolated and impenetrable to outside influences. Life in this community is full of opportunities to acquire, transmit, and/or combine a variety of cultural and linguistic resources.

The recognition perspective that we advocate owes much to the ethnographic stance that framed our research. This stance is characterized by an open-ended methodology known for focusing on that which is unexpected or new about the everyday lives of people. In adhering to this stance, we opened our minds to alternative interpretations about the conversations of Mexicano children and their families. As a result, we discovered how children and their family members draw upon knowledge about mainstream culture and the English language, as well as upon Mexican culture and Spanish. Rather than two or more competing cultural identities, we find a rich and creative borderland of interchanging identities of Mexicano, Latino, immigrant, Mexican American, Chicano, and American (Anzaldúa, 1987).

Although we focus on home and community practices, our findings provide a new foundation for assessing the school experiences of Mexicano children. As participants in a complex set of social relations, within and outside of their social networks, children from this community learn at an early age to appropriate and transform the knowledge at their disposal. They take what they learn in one context and use it in another, often as a place holder until they acquire the appropriate knowledge. When they are unable to meet the linguistic and cultural demands of social transactions, they enlist the assistance of others with more experience and skill. Among the families we studied, there was no reluctance to learn English, nor was there any resistance to mainstream cultural norms. Rather, family members actively sought solutions to problematic situations vis-à-vis a new culture and language by pooling available resources in the home and the community. Interactions within and outside the family repeatedly provided opportunities for children to treat language as an abstract entity, a skill some consider a hallmark of academic language use (Heath and Hoffman, 1986).

PUSHING BOUNDARIES: A CASE FOR INTERCULTURAL TRANSACTIONS

In the many interrelationships that exist throughout the community of social networks we call Eastside, language, whether English or Spanish, recognizes few borders.[4] Although visible markers of class, ethnicity, and residential patterns clearly demarcate areas as Stanford, Lincoln City, and the east side, both languages push through these sociocultural boundaries. The language of the commercial signs throughout the east side of Lincoln City – where we conducted our three studies – boldly announce the coexistence of various ethnolinguistic groups among which Anglo and Mexicano are the most prevalent. In the classrooms throughout the community, Spanish and English predominate over other languages in instructional and personal interactions. Even in the forested compounds of the nearby wealthy community of Concord, both languages may be heard as property owners and their mostly Mexicano staff interact.

Our work provides many instances in which the language experiences of the Mexicano children living in the east side are specific to life in an immigrant community: Children act as language and cultural brokers, rely heavily on oral knowledge sources, and engage in collaborative and cooperative language encounters. We also find, however, that the worlds of these students are not always clearly demarcated. A child's life in an ethnic community like Eastside contains opportunities to participate in a variety of activities where they acquire a wide range of cultural and linguistic resources. As mentioned earlier, these resources may reflect one or the other culture as well as a hybrid variety from their cross-cultural experiences.

In some situations, involving representatives from mainstream institutions, Eastside individuals, including children, must draw upon the knowledge of multiple cultures and languages. In other situations, Eastsiders engage in the same type of activity in the privacy of their homes as they attempt to uncover the tacit meanings of a second culture and language embedded in written or oral texts. During these occasions, which we call intercultural transactions, participants use multiple knowledge sources or languages to create meaning, negotiate a task, or solve a problem. For example, a child who translates for adults in her family's social networks engages in intercultural transactions. She operates from more than one cultural frame as she negotiates cross-language and same-language interactions within the same conversation using what she has learned in previous situations as tools for meaning-making. Whether it be in the privacy of their homes, around a text written in English, or in any of the many institutions with which Mexicanos conduct business, intercultural transactions bring to bear knowledge and language from different cultural backgrounds.

This book focuses on one of many subgroups that make up the Mexican origin population: Mexican immigrants who have lived in the United States for 20 years or less. In time, this group feeds into the Mexican origin population, one of the oldest and fastest growing ethnic groups in the United States. For example, it is estimated that Mexican immigrants make up approximately 80 percent of the 13.5 million Latinos in the United States who indicate Mexican ancestry in the 1991 census (Bureau of the U.S. Census).[5] In 1988, California Tomorrow, a policy organization, reported that almost a third of California's school-age population was language minority and of these 73 percent were Spanish-speaking. Because Mexican immigrants represent a majority among Latino immigrants, we can assume that a substantial number of these Spanish-speaking students are foreign born and/or come from Mexican immigrant families.[6] The children whose life and language we discuss in this book come from this student population, one which is expected to continue to grow and to present interesting and serious challenges to educators and policymakers.

Although we focus on a Mexican immigrant community in California, similar communities are scattered across the Southwest in such states as Colorado, Arizona, New Mexico, and Texas. As Luis Moll mentions in the foreword, Mexicanos are establishing new settlement patterns across the country. For generations Mexican immigrants have traveled northward on migratory arteries formed long before either Mexico or the United States became nations. They have settled in communities where friends, kin, or sometimes, *unos conocidos* (distant acquaintances), have previously established roots. These communities provide the recently arrived immigrants with elaborate networks of social relations operating on a culture and language similar to what they left back home in Mexico. These "ports of entry" provide immigrants with opportunities for work and integration into the mainstream of American culture.

Oral expression is one of the most significant areas in which Mexican immigrant communities in the United States reinforce patterns and practices common in the sending towns and villages of Mexico. The pervasiveness and significance of oral expression in the immigrant communities is well documented. Studies by anthropologists, folklorists, and sociolinguists (Paredes, 1958; Arora, 1972; Elías-Olivares, 1977; Peñalosa, 1978; McDowell, 1982; Elías-Olivares et al. 1985; Limón, 1986, in press; Delgado-Gaitan, 1990; Foley, 1990) depict a rich and complex language milieu in these homes and communities. For example, Ybarra-Frausto (1984) states that "the Chicano community affirms and validates a long-standing tradition of *buen hablar*" (p. 48) – the ability to use language effectively and in aesthetically pleasing ways. In face of the realities posed by immigrant life, "humor," a form of linguistic dexterity, says Ybarra-Frausto, "has allowed the Chicano to poke fun at adversity, to ridicule and laugh at his own social condition and thus to spiritually surmount his circumstances" (p. 45).

Our descriptions of the everyday talk that involves children and adults yields a multifaceted portrayal of the language socialization contexts available to Eastsiders. We focus on the ways in which children acquire and use knowledge and language from a variety of contexts to accomplish social and personal needs. This focus on everyday language ultimately allows us to hypothesize more meaningfully about how Mexicano children might be affected if their teachers were to use these children's background experience as the basis for classroom pedagogy (see Chapter 6).

This book is organized as follows. In Chapter 2, we outline the physical and social context which gives rise to the language activities that we describe. We find that children in Eastside learn language skills as much from members of their family's social networks (i.e., relatives, neighbors, and friends) as they do from their immediate family members. Socialization through language thus involves both the family-based interactions and exchanges in the broader social context in which children live and negotiate their needs. Children are often recruited by monolingual Spanish speakers or individuals not comfortable with their English fluency to participate in conversations that unravel the cultural and semantic underpinnings of written English texts and the Anglo world.

In Chapter 3, we focus on conversations that occurred in the context of two Eastside preschool-aged children's routine activities at home and at school. We highlight instances of the use of school language and/or school knowledge in the interactions between children and their adult interlocutors (parents and teachers) and lay the foundation for further development in later chapters of the notion of multiple knowledge and language sources used in intercultural transactions. In our description of a discourse device adults use with children, we show how Eastside adults take on a deliberate role in their children's language socialization. Although this particular discourse device has been described as one that tends not to be used by minority parents, we found that it was used by both Eastside parents and teachers.

The extent to which Mexicano children in Eastside have access to a variety of cultural and linguistic resources is explored in Chapter 4. We describe occasions when bilingual children draw on these resources in their personal and social interactions. In many cases, we find that these children are themselves resources that others draw upon to negotiate a second language and culture. We focus on two preadolescent bilingual children who demonstrate the linguistic adaptability and flexibility that is fostered through their bilingual and multicultural experiences in the community. One of these children, a child interpreter, for example, learns to treat language as an object to create meaning, to use technical terms and vocabulary in Spanish and English, and to assume the role and demeanor of an advocate.

In Chapter 5 we describe the analytic strategies children learn through observing and participating in extended family problem-solving discussions. These interpretive sessions focus on teasing out the meanings and underlying norms and expectations of a variety of texts. They show how nonnative speakers of English can successfully compensate for their lack of English skills and their unfamiliarity with mainstream culture. In many ways, these home-based language activities act as "prepping" sessions in which the petitioner is specifically equipped with a prepared document, a set of answers for probable questions, and a series of steps to follow in future intercultural communication. Additionally, these activities shed light on the role of literacy and literate behaviors in Mexicano homes.

Our work, like a growing body of social science research that relies on an ethnographic perspective, moves beyond the mere description of language activities to emphasize the academic potential of these home- and community-based language experiences. Teachers and researchers alike will find the descriptions of the linguistic and cultural practices of Mexicano immigrants a resource for innovative pedagogy and future research. In Chapters 6 and 7 we extend our work by specifying its pedagogical implications: The language experiences of Eastside children constitute a viable resource that can and should be incorporated into the instructional agenda. We present three examples of educational events – cross-age tutoring, after-school educational activities, and a two-way approach to bilingual education – that illustrate how linguistic and cultural practices can inform curriculum development and instructional strategies so that all participants operate in a collaborative, egalitarian context. We elaborate on our belief that home and community sources of knowledge should form an integral part of every level of instruction. We offer suggestions on how teachers can construct new knowledge within the context of integrated multiple perspectives, rather than on a single, monolithic and unrealistic perspective.

Chapter 2

Eastside: A Mexicano community[1]

The San Francisco Bay Area reaches 50 miles south into the fertile farming valleys of northern California. From San Francisco to San Jose on both sides of the bay, towns, cities, and subdivisions roll one upon another to form a seamless string of lights and sounds. Lincoln City lies in the center of the San Francisco peninsula. The community of Mexican immigrants that informs this book is part of an ethnic enclave located in roughly one square mile of unincorporated land that lies on Lincoln City's east side (see Figure 1). The east side is bounded by three major thoroughfares and the walled estates of the affluent city of Concord. Physically and socially, the east side stands visibly apart from the rest of Lincoln City. Not only does the social scene change from private to public as one comes into Lincoln City from Concord, but the language and physical characteristics of the residents change as well. The presence of the Mexicano community is obvious: The streets of the east side are alive with commercial and social activity in which the use of Spanish, both spoken and written, is as common as the use of English. Evidence of Mexican culture is easily discernible throughout the area in ways of dress, talk, and leisure. Although Lincoln City is more than 500 miles north of the U.S. and Mexican border, the commercial life of the east side looks remarkably similar to that of the Mexicano neighborhoods in such cities as Los Angeles, El Paso, or Tucson.

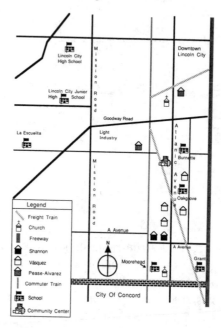

Figure 1. Map of Lincoln City.

To distinguish the Mexicano community from its geographical base (i.e., from the east side of Lincoln City) and to more accurately represent the permeability of its physical and social boundaries, we have named the community "Eastside" (See Figure 2). Eastside gains its life and vitality from a fusion of multiple communities. It is bounded by patterns of contact between individuals who share similar cultural and familial backgrounds and who participate in elaborate relations of exchange (Keefe and Padilla, 1987)[2] that extend throughout California and into regions as far away as Mexico, Oregon, and Washington. Our observations and our descriptions focus on the part of the community that is situated on the east side of Lincoln City.

For many Mexicanos the east side is the port of entry into American culture and institutions. In this chapter we give a brief historical and social sketch of the sociocultural contexts that shape the group's patterns of language use and language learning, which, in turn, provides a framework for

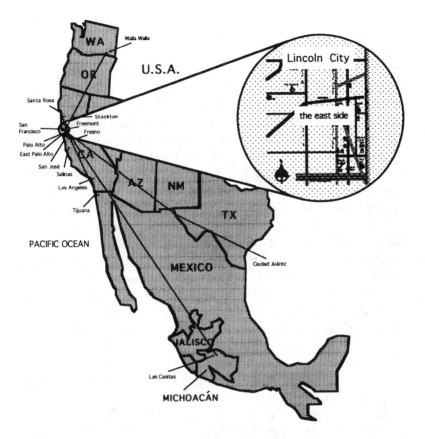

Figure 2. Map of the Eastside community in its larger context.

examining the home and community-based cultural and linguistic resources available to the children and their families.

The influence of Mexicano culture on Lincoln City dates
back to when the area was part of Rancho de las Plumas, a
very large parcel of land owned by the Montoya family in the
early nineteenth century. At the turn of the twentieth century, Lincoln City, like many other California cities, attracted
numerous immigrants who came to work for the railroad
(Galarza, 1971). Portuguese, Italian, and Spanish immigrants settled in company housing situated on the east side
of the city as did Mexicans. As one resident, Mrs. Nuñez,

21

remarked, *"Nunca faltaron Mexicanos. Uno que el otro."* ["There has never been a lack of Mexicans. One here or there."] She came from Mexico in the 1940s with her husband, who joined the railroad laborers. Over the past 30 years, the demography of the region has been changing dramatically. In addition to pockets of Anglo middle- and working-class homes, the area now includes enclaves of immigrants from Southern Europe, Latin America, the Pacific Islands, and Mexico. Among these nonnative groups, immigrants from Mexico are the most numerous. In the second half of the 1980s, during the time that we were each involved in the field work discussed in this book, it was estimated that over 40 percent of the east side's population was Mexicano (*Lincoln City Times*, February, 1988).[3]

For most of the 1980s Mexican influence predominated, but it did not obliterate the presence of other ethnic groups. Anglos, African Americans, and immigrants from Asia and the Pacific Rim could be observed throughout the downtown area. Restaurants on the east side offered a variety of cuisines besides Mexican food. For example, a Chinese cafe operated next door to Mrs. Nuñez's restaurant, across the street was a Vietnamese establishment, and a Salvadorean restaurant was situated two blocks north. The Anglo residents for the most part congregated at a coffee shop on Atlantic Avenue. The area's residential neighborhoods displayed a high concentration of various ethnic/racial groups such as Samoans, Tongans, African Americans, Filipinos, and Latin Americans. This multi-ethnic concentration was not a characteristic of the surrounding neighborhoods of Concord and Lincoln City, where Anglos were the majority.

Many residential street scenes on the east side also signaled a strong Mexican influence. Along Atlantic Avenue, a main street at the southernmost end of the east side, local grocery store windows were plastered with advertisements for such items as *tortillas, queso, leche,* and *chiles* [tortillas, cheese, milk, and chilis]. Shops like *la zapatería* [the shoe store], *las tienditas* ["Mom and Pop" markets], *restaurantes* [restaurants], *joyerías* [jewelry stores], and *discotecas* [record stores] all advertised in Spanish. Businesses in the area often catered to the regional tastes of immigrants from the central Mexican highlands state of Michoacán, which is the sending state for a substantial number of Eastside's Mexicano immigrants (Fonseca and Moreno, 1984).[4] The *catarinas* [catering vans] stationed strategically along Atlantic Avenue sold grilled-meat tacos served with onions, chili peppers, and slices of lime, *al estilo Michoacán* [Michoacán style]. Other businesses, like the barber shop, the car upholstery, painting, and repair shops, and the furniture stores, supplied products and services catering especially to a Spanish-speaking clientele.

Peddlers selling produce and other food items door-to-door, a rarity in other neighborhoods of Lincoln City, were a familiar sight in the east side. The *paletero* [ice-cream vendor] and the *panadero* [baker] came through the neighborhood regularly. Their arrival was typically heralded by the children, who requested spare change from their parents. As one mother put it, *"Mi hija mantiene al paletero."* ["My daughter supports the ice-cream vendor."][5] Products such as clothing, textiles, and jewelry imported from Mexico, as well as a multitude of homemade food items, including *tamales* [corn-meal dish], *chorizo* [Mexican sausage], and tacos, were easily available from peddlers and part-time merchants who operated from their homes. On Sunday mornings, the living rooms of several residents in the area were transformed into restaurants featuring *tacos de carne asada* [barbecue tacos], *pozole* [hominy-beef soup], or *menudo* [tripe soup]. Other neighbors specialized in crocheted items, children's clothing, or kitchen items, all imported from Mexico over time on a small-scale, individual basis.

Some Mexicanos living in the east side call their area a "barrio," by which they mean, literally, a neighborhood:

> Esta área ya es un barrio mexicano. Ahora muchos de los negocios incluyen sobre todo, restaurantes, bares, cantinas, esos

carros que venden tacos, paletas. Bueno es completamente una colonia mexicana. Porque si alguien hace pan en su casa lo anda ofreciendo en las calles igual que en Mexico. Andan con carritos de paletas y andan en las calles.

This area already is a Mexican barrio. Now many businesses include, above all, restaurants, bars, cantinas, those carts that sell tacos, popsicles. Well, it is completely a Mexican colony. Because if someone makes bread at home, they go around selling it in the streets the same as in Mexico. They go around with popsicle carts and go around in the streets.

We argue, however, that the east side is not a barrio as typically defined in the social science literature, where the word connotes sections of towns and cities where Latino and working-class residents are socially, economically, and residentially segregated (Camarillo, 1979). Social scientists also have used the concept of barrio to indicate a section of town whose Mexican identity and character reflect strong historical roots. Many barrios described in the social science literature were originally established in the wake of the Spanish and Mexican colonization of the west and survived the encroachment of other ethnic groups. The area we examine is not the "Barrio East Side" in the same sense that Barrio Maravilla of Los Angeles, Barrio Logan of San Diego, and Barrio El Segundo of El Paso are barrios. These barrios share features that distinguish them from other neighborhoods: They lie within the confines of physical boundaries such as freeways or railroad tracks and are residentially and socially segregated neighborhoods.[6] Although the east side of Lincoln City is sharply segregated from the affluent Anglo communities to its west and south by similar boundaries (freeway, railroad tracks, and walls of the Concord estates), the Mexicano community we call Eastside is not *contained within these boundaries*. In fact, the immediate community extends out into neighboring communities, not infrequently into the forested Concord estates where friends or relatives live and work as live-in maids and groundsmen. Moreover, the area has only relatively recently become a notable base for the Mexicano immigrant population. Although Mexicanos have always been present in the east side area, they began coming in significant numbers in the 1960s. As one long-time Eastside resident told us, "Cuando vinimos en 1964 éramos los únicos mexicanos viviendo en esta calle." ["When we came in 1964 we were the only Mexicans living on this street."][7]

The east side also lacks another characteristic that the social science literature defines as an essential aspect of a barrio: It has not been labeled by its residents with a name that distinguishes it from the rest of Lincoln City. Instead, the residents simply say that they live in Lincoln City. Some indicate the area of town they come from, but only social institutions and the school refer to the area as "the east side." In contrast, residents of El Barrio, a Puerto Rican barrio in New York City, refer to their *bloque* [block] according to the street number or according to team or social club names – for example, Los Gavilanes from 104th (Zentella, 1980). Similarly, in the East Los Angeles barrio, the neighborhoods all have names: Maravilla, Whitefence, Belvedere, Boyle Heights, and so on. In the following litany by Raúl R. Salinas (1972), the Chicano poet expresses the intimate connection between a barrio, its name, and its people:

My Loma of Austin
My Rose Hill of Los Angeles
My Westside of San Anto
My Quinto of Houston
My Jackson of San Jo
My Segundo of El Paso
My Barelas of Albuquerque
My Westside of Denver

Flats, Los Marcos, Maravilla, Calle Guadalupe,
Magnolia, Buena Vista, Mateo, La Seis, Chiquis, El
Sur, and all Chicano neighborhoods that now exist
and once existed; somewhere . . . someone
remembers . . .

The lack of a single name for the east side emphasizes the relative youth of the neighborhood as a Mexicano/Latino community. It also emphasizes the heterogeneity and fluidity of the area, where, as already noted, the Mexicano community is but one of many ethnic groups. It is unlikely that the future development of the east side of Lincoln City will follow the patterns noted in the growth of barrios elsewhere: High property values make it very difficult for Mexicanos to establish permanent roots on the east side.

The Mexicanos of the community we call Eastside are part of a discernible network of social relations. The bonds that form this virtual community are cultural and linguistic and extend north, south, and east as represented in Figure 2. Class and regional background also have a strong influence on the definition of this community. Most Mexicanos of Eastside are working-class, first-generation immigrants and speak Spanish as their first language. Most have been in the United States less than 20 years. Since the 1960s, newly arrived Mexicano immigrants have flocked to available housing behind both sides of the business strip along Atlantic Avenue.

Throughout this time, large extended families, single families, and individual immigrants have inhabited an assortment of low-income housing – single-family bungalows, duplexes, apartment buildings, and federally funded condominiums on the east side. Initially, the presence of already established family and compatriots, as well as socioeconomic factors (e.g., limited English language ability and little formal education), predisposed many immigrants to settle in low-income areas such as the east side. Rents were less costly there than in other parts of Lincoln City, but they were not cheap. In the 1980s many small two-bedroom dwellings rented from $550 to $750 per month. These small homes frequently housed large extended families and *arrimados* [boarders] who pooled their financial resources to meet household expenses. When families could afford to leave their overcrowded conditions – or were forced out by landlords – they tended to settle in housing close to other members of their social networks (Galarza, 1971). Yet, it was not uncommon for established residents to move to other geographic regions far from friends and other family members where real estate was less expensive.

In the 1980s, the Mexicano community in the east side was clearly working-class. For recent immigrants, the obstacles to obtaining employment were many. Oral language skills in English were essential, but literacy skills, sometimes in both languages, were required for better jobs, and by law, all immigrants needed proof of their legal status in order to secure jobs in the United States. Obviously, Mexicano men and women were employed without being able to meet these requirements, but the few positions available to non-English-speaking and undocumented workers were also the least desirable. Low-skilled jobs as day laborers and domestics in hotels and private homes required little or no English and often no proof of legal status. Domestic work was the second-highest employment category for women (housewife was the first).[8] Men were most likely to be employed in the service sector, as unskilled janitors, gardeners, and kitchen helpers. Jobs in fast-food restaurants, retail bargain stores, and factories were more competitive and tended to be held by young people who had attended school in the United States and who had acquired some fluency in English and some literacy skills.

For many Eastsiders simply making ends meet entailed ingenuity and collective effort. For example, Mr. Delgado was self-employed as a construction worker. He maintained a small crew that constantly changed personnel as workers came and went. Mrs. Delgado often worked with her husband when the crew dwindled or when the Delgados needed to maximize profits. Shortage of work was a constant problem, as was establishing contacts with contractors. The jobs Mr. Delgado was able to secure were often brief and technically nondemanding, a combination that not only curtailed income but also forced Mr. Delgado to venture further into the English-speaking business world, where he could not work legally. The work experiences of the Macías family are further evidence of the routine struggles of many Mexicanos. Mr. and Mrs. Macías each suffered back injuries as a result of their work (he as a janitor and she as a kitchen helper) and both were forced to quit and rely on workers' compensation. Although the insurance company's lawyers suspected that the couple was attempting to "live off the system," Mr. and Mrs. Macías actually were desperately looking for ways to earn more money because the workers' compensation payments were insufficient. Mr. Macías and his eldest son, Adán, sold flowers on the streets throughout the Bay Area until Mr. Macías was "caught" working. Even then, the Macías family was not without resources: They had the advantage of a large social network that provided support when the efforts of individual families or family members failed.

Despite the obstacles of language, culture, and economics, many immigrant families, in time, managed to raise themselves above poverty-level conditions. Thus, by the time we conducted our case studies, the east side's Mexicano community was no more financially homogeneous than it was culturally or linguistically so. The entrepreneurs who owned the taco trucks, those who organized construction and gardening crews, and those workers who held down two jobs usually could generate enough money to buy a home and live a relatively comfortable life. Achieving economic stability and competing for more skilled jobs was an obvious trend in the community. Typically, families began to be more successful as they gained legal status and as their children reached working-age equipped with higher levels of education, greater fluency in English, and more sophisticated literacy skills. Mrs. Macías' brother-in-law, for example, worked his way up to a managerial position in an exterminating company, an achievement directly tied to his English language proficiency, among other factors. He bought a house on the west side of Lincoln City and sent his two young daughters to a Catholic elementary school, where he paid full tuition.

PATTERNS OF LANGUAGE USE

Eastside's Mexicano community is characterized by a dynamic exchange of cultures, languages, and social classes. Besides the choice of language, community life offers a variety of ways for using language related to the presence of both Mexican and Anglo cultures. Information about the world outside the context of Eastsider's social networks is brought into the home through the media, experiences in the work place, and the children's experiences at school. These outside contacts make new sources of knowledge and different uses of language available to the residents. Through a complex set of intra- and intercultural transactions, the Mexicano community becomes "increasingly fluent in an Anglo cultural milieu at the same time that they become more fluent in a local Mexican culture" (Rosaldo, 1985, p. 12). The families maintain their own cultural and linguistic repertoire while incorporating and enhancing new ways of speaking garnered from their intercultural experiences. At home and in the community, relatives and friends engage in lengthy discussions about knowledge from their multicultural world. In these discussions, the families demonstrate the oral virtuosity that the Mexican culture encourages (Ybarra-Frausto, 1984). They extend, interpret, critique, and appropriate new knowledge that enters their lives. Individuals retell or compose anew stories, jokes, and poetry for the entertainment of family members. Common themes for discussion in these homes include family history, personal incidents, folklore, and recent events in the media. Nicknames frequently are assigned that incite playful banter between individuals. At a more serious level, family members exchange knowledge of various kinds in the routine execution of daily chores and activities (Moll, 1992).

At home many language activities center around situations in which the activity itself is a source of knowledge. Watching a television program, for example, might prompt brief analytical discussions among family members. Similarly, watching television sometimes offers children an opportunity to hone their skills as translators. Although most of the T.V. programs adult members of Eastside watch are broadcast in Spanish, when adults view English-language broadcasts, they typically ask the bilingual children who are present to interpret.

In private conversations family members abstract and manipulate knowledge while talking about their encounters in everyday life. These situations mainly involve printed materials, such as homework, job applications, and other official forms, which by their nature often require the individuals to find the meaning in the text, to fill in blank spaces, and/or to write extended passages for an unknown audience. Mexicano children and adults commonly pool their resources to meet the challenge of a printed text that requires them to divulge information and demonstrate knowledge. For example, Rosa, a bilingual teenager who frequently acted as the family's translator, relied not only on her own skills, but also on the linguistic and knowledge bases of those present during a family discussion, to assist her cousin in answering questions on the latter's tax data form (see Chapter 3).

Perhaps the most significant characteristic of Eastside's linguistic repertoire – the element of choice – is concisely described by twelve-year-old Sal Mora, a lifetime resident of the east side.[9] He observed that children rely on both of their languages when conversing with one another. "Whatever they're used to," he explained. "If you're used to speaking English, they'll speak English. If one speaks English but the other one is used to speaking Spanish – they'll speak Spanish. That's all there is to it." Then he added, "Sometimes you don't know 'til you do it." The choice of one language over the other may lead to further choices. For example, while Mexican Spanish is most common at home and in conversation with other Eastsiders, several different varieties of Spanish are also spoken on the east side. On one occasion, two middle-school girls pointed out that a boy from El Salvador used the *vosotros* form of you (the plural "you"), usage common in El Salvador but not in Mexico. Regional variations of Mexican Spanish also are evident. For example, one woman made a distinction between the two terms used for "tomato": *jitomate* and *tomate*. She explained that, at least in the area of Mexico from which she came, *tomate* referred to fresh tomatoes and *jitomate* to cooked or canned ones.

Children also have many opportunities to come in contact with English. English typically is spoken during interethnic communication with outside institutions such as schools and other public and private service agencies. Some children's initial contact with English occurs at school. For others, English is introduced by their older siblings, either during play or through direct instruction. One teenager, for example, taught her preschool-aged sister how to ask the teacher if she could go to the bathroom. The tutoring amused the rest of the family, who laughed and applauded the little girl's efforts. As their bilingual abilities increase, Eastside children tend to use both English and Spanish. Adults frequently rely on children to serve as interpreters, thus extending the youngster's contacts with English while also enhancing and maintaining their use of Spanish.

INTRACULTURAL COMMUNICATION

The patterns of language use we observed in the east side emerge from the interplay between two sociocultural contexts: communication within and outside of the cultural group. We begin our analysis with the former. Culture is fostered through participation in community life, as manifested in interactions among the social networks of kin, compatriots, and friends who make up the community (Rosaldo, 1985; Vélez-Ibañez and Greenberg, 1992). These local networks serve several purposes. Members supply child care, transportation, and entertainment; some also act as mediators vis-à-vis outside institutions. Equally important, however, is the role that these networks play in providing

31

members with socioemotional and physical security. Mrs. Neruda, for example, explained that she remained on the east side, even though that meant putting up with her ex-husband's intrusions, because of the secure sense of community she derived from her family-based social network. For similar reasons, Mrs. Cristóbal refused to rent a house outside of the area after her home burned down.[10] Although it is clear that finances, educational training, English fluency, and cultural ties restricted their mobility, the two women depended on relatives and friends to help them meet the demands of daily life, and this dependence was their primary motive for staying in the area. As such examples suggest, some of the Mexicano families we encountered in our field studies centered their social lives around networks that were restricted to immediate or extended family. Other families, however, who were more integrated into the social and cultural activities of the Mexicano community, extended their social networks to include the families of newly acquired friends (e.g., the families of members of a soccer team, a church group, or a folkloric dance troupe).

Participating in each others' religious and secular celebrations offers many opportunities for network members to meet and exchange information about their lives and about the lives of relatives still in Mexico. Similarly, traditional fiestas for baptisms, birthdays, *quinceañeras* [debutante parties for fifteen-year-old girls], and weddings provide occasions for families to congregate with their relatives and friends and reinforce cultural values and norms. For example, the planning of fiestas, as shown in Figure 3 on the preparation of cracklings, helps perpetuate the community's culture at the same time that it requires the families to interact with Anglo institutions. These interactions form the basis for discussions concerning the procedures and cultural expectations that are associated with the specific social functions being planned. A baptism is one such celebration. Family members must negotiate the procedures for officiating the

Figure 3. Preparing cracklings for a family fiesta.

religious and secular aspects of the ceremony with such institutions as the local recreation center, whose hall is a popular site for family gatherings. In one family Vásquez observed, members relied heavily on family customs for guidance regarding the sacred and the secular components of a baptism. Godparents as well as parents knew ahead of time what their roles required of them. Conventional practices relegated *Padrinos* [Godparents] to pay part of the expenses and purchase the child's baptism gown as shown in Figure 4. To maneuver through the church bureaucracy, family members often profited from bits and pieces of information shared by others who had previous experience with events surrounding the organization of a baptism.

Eastsiders have access to Mexican cultural knowledge from a variety of sources outside the home. Many commercial services available in the community are provided by

Figure 4. Padrino and godchild after baptism.

compatriots, who cater to specific preferences for foods, plants, music, and clothing.[11] Equally important, however, is the valuable cultural role these entrepreneurs play, acting as a conduit for traditional knowledge. For example, traditional folkways of transmitting knowledge orally are reinforced during occasions of folk healing by *la sobadora* [masseuse] or *el curandero* [healer]; during the distribution of goods by vendors such as *el paletero* [the ice-cream pushcart peddler] and *los que venden tacos de las catarinas* [those who sell tacos from the catering trucks]; and from members of the social network who possess specialized knowledge (e.g., an auto mechanic, a sheet rock specialist, and a leader of *novenas* [nine-day Catholic prayer rituals]). Additional informal sources for transmitting the old culture include *la chismosa* [gossiper] and *el panadero* [the baker], both of whom routinely broadcast news throughout the neighborhood.

Figure 5. Mexican visitor mourns the violent death of his brother.

The gossiper concentrates on passing along news concerning the personal lives of *conocidos* [acquaintances]; the *panadero*, who sells his bread from house to house, carries less mundane news, likely to appeal to a wider audience (e.g., reporting details of an accident that decimated a Latin American soccer team).

Certain individuals in the community play an especially important role in maintaining language patterns brought from the old country. Doña María, a popular *sobadora* [masseuse], shared her knowledge in intimate consultations with adults who came from as far as Oregon to see her. While she practiced her medicine, she informed her patients (or in some case, their parents) about child-rearing practices, nutrition, and traditional ways of life. On one occasion, while she lifted *la mollera* [the fontanel] of a toddler, she explained to the child's mother why it had fallen and instructed her on how and what to feed the baby. She also counseled the mother on how to protect the child from the elements. Doña Luisa, also well-known among members of Eastside, provided an essential socioreligious function.[12] When she heard about a death, she approached the affected family and volunteered to lead a *novena* in honor of the deceased. For nine consecutive days, she led the family in prayers; she also provided an opportunity before and after the prayers for members of the family to engage in discussions far removed from the tragedy they had experienced (see Figure 5, a photograph of family members gathered for a funeral). Consequently, she both helped the family ease the pain of death and perpetuated a traditional function within the structure of their cultural heritage. She explained her role eloquently:

> . . . uno debe pedir por ellas [almas en purgatorio] para que ellas pidan a Dios por nosotros y a uno las creencias que sus padres le enseñaron, a uno nunca se le olvidan.

> . . . one ought to pray for them [souls in purgatory] so that they can petition god in our favor and [also so] one does not forget the beliefs our parents have taught us.

Despite the efforts of women such as Doña Maria and Doña Luisa to perpetuate traditional beliefs and ways of dealing with knowledge, Mexicano children raised in American society frequently reject roles and activities associated with their cultural heritage. Although children are familiar with many of these practices, their cultural reference has faded. At best, the gestures become social events. Leti Macías, for example, was willing to oblige her mother by placing flowers at the foot of the statue of the Virgen de Guadalupe only after her friend agreed to accompany her. School-aged children are conspicuously absent from the novenas and the masseuse's waiting room. Doña Luisa lamented that none of her own 12 children led the novenas. She comforted herself, however, with the fact that her children knew the socioreligious conventions governing novenas even though they did not practice them.

INTERCULTURAL COMMUNICATION

The culture and the language of the host country are typically acquired more formally than those of the heritage country, usually through intercultural communication that occurs outside the home and community. The exigencies of everyday life require that most, if not all, members of Eastside's Mexicano community interact with members of other groups, especially Anglos. Most of these interactions with Anglos are hierarchical, instrumental, and short-term. Because of language, education, and social class, the Mexicano inevitably bargains from a subordinate position, whether he or she requests a service or provides one. Such intercultural encounters typically are official in nature, in contrast to the socially motivated episodes of intracultural communication. Outside of teachers and neighbors Anglos rarely receive invitations to join Eastside Mexicano families in their many celebrations, signaling the distance between the two groups.

The most basic intercultural communication often takes place with little oral language. Paying bills or purchasing such items as groceries, gas, and stamps can be accomplished with very little verbal interaction. Intercultural communication that involves more than the basic exchange of goods or services requires cultural and linguistic skills and knowledge specific to the mainstream institutional culture. Effective outcomes depend on individuals' accumulated skills in these areas. For example, executing bureaucratic details such as filling out job applications, applying for immigration status, loans, and licenses, receiving public services, or soliciting services from institutions such as banks, schools, or medical offices, often require the additional services of individuals who speak English and who have had previous experience with the particular institution. When literacy is involved, the paperwork is often taken home, where the assistance of a family or community interpreter is solicited. Children frequently are pulled out of school to act as language and cultural brokers for family members or friends.

When translation resources within the social network are exhausted, families seek professional assistance from a local service agency. Occasionally, agencies provide a professional interpreter or translator when one is required by law.

Due to their nonresident status, Eastsiders must engage in a variety of complicated transactions with representatives of mainstream institutions – e.g., courts, immigration authorities, and the Internal Revenue Service. The 1986 Immigration Reform and Control Act (IRCA), which offered amnesty to previously undocumented individuals who had entered the United States prior to 1982, dramatically affected the number of intercultural transactions in the Mexicano community. Amnesty applicants were required to prove that they had lived in the United States undocumented prior to 1982 or to prove that they had worked in agricultural jobs for a specified period of time. Like their counterparts nationwide, Eastside Mexicanos were forced to engage in transactions with many institutions – schools, former employers, hospitals, and various public agencies – to request documentation that could be used as evidence to establish their long-term residence in the United States. Amnesty changed the legal status of many individuals in Eastside, making it possible for them to travel to and from Mexico, hold legal employment, and apply for social services.[13]

There is no way to know precisely how many Eastside residents applied for and received amnesty, but one indication comes from the first organized community meeting that took place shortly after the law passed. The organizers of a grassroots group called *El Comité en Defensa de Los Inmigrantes* [The Committee in Defense of the Immigrants] joked openly about how few people they expected to show up at the meeting. Because most people who would be likely to qualify for amnesty intensely distrusted the U.S. Immigration and Naturalization Service (INS), committee organizers anticipated that most residents would boycott the meeting on the presumption that it was simply a set-up that would result in *una redada* [a raid]. Nevertheless, over 400 people attended that first meeting.

Individual members of the Mexicano community achieved their goals in intercultural encounters with varying rates of success. For example, an entire family's amnesty applications were held up for months because the family did not understand how to proceed in acquiring various forms required by the law after the school system refused to provide proof of their children's attendance. Another family frequently sought medical attention as far away as Tijuana, Mexico, because they consistently found the diagnosis and treatment received from local medical facilities unsatisfactory. As one parent put it, *"Yo le perdí la fe a estos doctores cuando no le encontraban nada a ella."* ["I lost faith in these doctors when they didn't find anything wrong with her (his wife)"].[14] On another occasion, a mother took steps to enroll all of her children in a private school when her request for the transfer of one of her children from one teacher to another was denied by the principal of the local public school. Mrs. Zapata complained to the principal that her child was not learning to read from a particular teacher.[15] The principal, believing that the teacher's pedagogical orientation was sound, declined the request. Confident that her intuitions were correct, Mrs. Zapata applied for enrollment of her three daughters in a local parochial school. Because the children were monolingual Spanish speakers and could not pass the entrance exams, admission was denied. These interactions are indications of the many difficulties and challenges that intercultural communications frequently pose for Mexicanos of Eastside.

EASTSIDE SCHOOLS

Eastside schools play an important role in children's second language acquisition and in their formal introduction to mainstream culture and institutions. For the children, schools represent a source of sustained and intricate intercultural communication. The elementary schools on the east side of Lincoln City are part of a larger school district which, like many in California, has undergone tremendous demographic change. The Anglo student population has been decreasing steadily for the last 20 years. The Lincoln City Elementary School District served over 15 different ethnic groups at the time of our field studies. Despite this apparent diversity, however, the schools were overwhelmingly Mexicano/Latino: According to district records, in the 1980s Hispanics made up well over 80 percent of the school-age population in three of the east side's elementary schools. By the late 1980s nearly 50 percent of the student population was classified Hispanic.[16]

A vast majority of Mexicano children on the east side do not do well in school. In the 1980s, the high school drop out rate for Mexicano/Latino students was about 50 percent. These students perform well below both national and district-wide norms on achievement tests. Their school grades are no more heartening: While 60 percent of the Anglo high school student population in the district earns A's and B's, only 38 percent of the students categorized as Hispanic, most of whom live on the east side of Lincoln City, receive these grades (*The Peninsula Times Tribune*, May 12, 1991). The reasons underlying this lack of achievement are complex. Our research suggests that at the very least, "deficit" conceptions of the academic potential of Mexicano students should be abandoned. As our work documents, much about the life of Eastside Mexicanos attests to their resourcefulness, concern for their children, and ability to adapt to unfamiliar and difficult situations.

Over the years, the district has mandated curricular reforms aimed at improving the academic circumstances of students from the east side. Of these reforms, bilingual education is probably the most controversial. The first bilingual program was established in 1970 at Morehead Elementary school (see Figure 1 for location of schools). It was not until 1980, however, that the district manifested a real commitment to bilingual education. In a 1981 report to the Lincoln City Elementary District School Board, the director of bilingual education argued that the following three events were evidence of the district's commitment:

1. The school district shares the costs of bilingual education with the state and federal government.
2. The school district established a policy stating that bilingual education was the instructional approach to be used for meeting the needs of limited English-speaking children.
3. The school district established a hiring policy stating that preference would be given to hiring certified bilingual/bicultural teachers.

During the 1980s, the bilingual programs in schools on the east side concentrated on providing children with instructional support in their native language while developing their English. Although maintaining and further developing minority children's native language was not a stated goal of the program, the school district consistently employed teachers and administrators who supported this goal. In 1988, a group of these teachers and administrators drafted a district-wide plan advocating the maintenance and development of Spanish for all students regardless of ethnic background. The plan, however, was not approved by the board.

Bilingual education has faced challenges throughout its history in the Lincoln City Elementary School District. Opponents maintain that the schools have a mandate to teach English; doing otherwise, they argue, would seriously jeopardize students' access to mainstream curriculum and would undermine their economic and social advancement. Parents of Mexicano/Latino children sometimes worry that children enrolled in bilingual classes will not learn English.[17] Other parents have not been pleased by the quality of instruction in bilingual classes and by the teachers' Spanish language abilities. Parents often complained of teachers' incorrect Spanish on written texts sent home and repeatedly referred to teachers' oral fluency as "mocho" [broken]. Finally, many teachers without bilingual/bicultural certification have opposed the district's policy to hire and tenure only fully certified bilingual/bicultural teachers.

The recent move to school-based management represents another significant district reform. In the mid-1980s, Lincoln City's schools began to seek their own solutions to their students' academic plight. Each school made efforts to incorporate specific instructional practices or approaches; some even identified themselves with a particular approach or set of instructional practices. For example, starting in the late 1970s, the staff at Oakgrove Elementary School began exploring alternative approaches to literacy education. Led by the resource teacher at the school, teachers began to read books about schools with similar problems and thus began to consult with educational experts. One expert, Arlene Brown, had developed a successful psycholinguistic reading program at a nearby school that inspired the Oakgrove staff. Building on Brown's model of insisting that students devote long periods of time to reading, the Oakgrove teachers set aside one hour per day when fourth, fifth, and sixth graders would read books of their choice. Within one year's time, the children scored between 1.1 and 1.8 years of growth in reading on the California Test of Basic Skills (CTBS), as opposed to the 4 to 6 months of growth they had made in previous years. This success helped the faculty obtain a grant from a local business to implement a whole language approach to literacy instruction at Oakgrove. The school used the grant money to purchase books to be used in classrooms and to hire educational consultants who worked directly with classroom teachers.

Other schools, too, tried new practices and approaches. Burnett Elementary School adopted the accelerated approach to instruction advocated by Professor Henry Levin of Stanford University. Grant Elementary School concentrated on providing staff members with special training in cooperative modes of organizing instruction promoted by another Stanford University professor, Elizabeth Cohen. All schools retained a commitment to bilingual education. At least two classes per grade level in each school were formally designated bilingual classes where Spanish was the medium of instruction for at least a portion of the school day.

In general, the schools have been much less innovative in establishing ties with the students' homes and communities. The district and local schools' failure to successfully engage the community reveals a lack of understanding not only of the residents' needs, but of the reality of their lives. For example, the district distributes a bilingual newsletter periodically, but this form of communication is of questionable value in homes where reading and writing skills are limited or nonexistent. Vásquez, for example, found that some parents in the four households she studied did not read or write either English or Spanish. Similarly, the schools had few programs or mechanisms which were designed to involve monolingual Spanish-speaking parents in planning or policy decisions. Existing structures, like parent meetings and parent advisory councils, which have historically been effective in drawing Anglo parents into the schooling process, have not proven useful or have been short-lived. Few Mexicano/Latino parents participated in meetings and advisory councils. Moreover, there was little direct communication between the schools and Mexicano/Latino parents. In most cases, it was the children who acted as go-betweens, conveying the intentions and goals of the schools to their parents and transmitting their parents' concerns and questions to the school staff.

Despite their lack of direct involvement in school affairs, Mexicano parents are interested in what goes on in their children's schools. As their collective response to numerous policy and instructional decisions by the schools and the district indicate, these parents also have strong allegiance to their neighborhood schools. One example of this loyalty is the community's opposition to the 1978 school board decision to close Morehead Elementary School. The board favored closure for several reasons: It would reduce the district's costs, which had risen in the wake of Proposition 13's cutbacks to schools; the building needed repairs; enrollment was declining; and redistributing Morehead's student body would bring the district into closer conformity with state guidelines regarding minority isolation. Parents vigorously opposed the closure and moved swiftly and effectively to keep Morehead open. Over 200 people attended the last of a series of three public hearings on the issue. Parents eventually exerted sufficient pressure to overturn the school board's decision. As the PTA president explained, "It is the contention of the parents at Morehead school that the present decline in enrollment is temporary – both because of an average increase in the birthrate, and most especially due to the lower costs of homes in the area, which will bring more families into this community." She noted as well that the community at large did not want to lose its neighborhood school, which served as the only park accessible to the children, provided a bilingual and bicultural environment reflecting that of its community, and promoted special programs to meet the neighborhood's cultural and economic needs. Parents also worried that closing neighborhood schools would force their children to attend schools located outside of the community, on the other side of the railroad tracks. At issue was their children's safety as they crossed tracks that were part of a main-line, rapid-transit route (see Figure 1, p. 20).

A similar mobilization effort on the part of the community characterized more recent events at La Escuelita, a preschool facility at Burnett Elementary School. In 1990, parents concerned about clashes between the new director of the preschool and a well-liked head teacher responded by boycotting the school. More than half of the families were represented at a meeting facilitated – at the request of parents – by a local mediator. These parents expressed their frustration with recent events at the school and with the seeming indifference of the new director. Differences between the director and head teacher were temporarily smoothed over, but parents and staff continued to have difficulties communicating with the director. On several occasions, parents formally expressed their concern and dissatisfaction to the preschool's Board of Directors. Parents also increased their representation on the board from one to four members. The director resigned after a year-and-a-half.

As the Mexicano community of Eastside attempts to make its own way in U.S. society, community members make use of all the cultural and linguistic resources available to them. Theirs is not a separate community, but one that is part of a web of multiple and interacting communities. The life experiences of Mexicanos in Eastside, including the skills they acquire in literacy and language use, are shaped by the rich and varied intra- and intercultural transactions that are a normal and necessary part of everyday life. Understanding the uses and development of language and literacy in this kind of a community requires a recognition of this dynamic interplay.

Chapter 3

Home and school contexts for language learning

Yo hago cosas que ayudan a mi hijo a desarrollar su lenguaje.
Le nombro los productos que encontramos en la tienda. Le
doy palabritas que no sabe cuando expresa sus ideas. Y siempre conversamos.

Rosa Hernández

I do things that help my son to develop his language. I name
the products that we find at the store. I tell him words that
he doesn't know when he expresses his ideas. And we always talk.

In the preceding quote, Rosa Hernández, a Mexican immigrant from a working-class background, recounts a
common theme in the literature on children's language development: language learning as a negotiated activity.[1] This
perspective is routinely supported using evidence from
studies on the language-learning environments available to
middle-class, English-speaking students. These studies portray middle-class homes as places where parents initiate
conversations with their children and adjust their own conversation to make it more accessible to their children. They
elicit clarifications and elaborations, expand and extend
children's utterances, and regularly engage children in predictable conversational routines (Brown and Bellugi, 1964;
Ratner and Bruner, 1977; Ninio and Bruner, 1977; Snow,

46

1977, 1983; Cazden, 1979; Scollon and Scollon, 1981). Evidence from ethnographic research suggests that the language learning environment of ethnic minority children from working-class populations living in the United States is quite different from that of white middle-class children. In the minority communities authors such as Miller (1982), Heath (1983), Boggs (1985), and Philips (1983) studied, adults didn't engage children in extended conversations or accommodate their speech to their children's developmental level. Instead of building upon children's previous talk by asking for additional information, elaborating, or paraphrasing, adults from these communities relied on non-accommodative discourse patterns (e.g., modeling, directives, infrequent use of expansions and questions) when they talked with children. Moreover, adult family members do not always appear to be the most significant participants in children's language development. Several researchers have shown that the language experiences of children in the minority communities they studied were dominated by peer interactions.

These observed empirical differences have been used to support the controversial cultural-difference and home-school mismatch theory, which asserts that the educational plight of ethnic minority students results from a lack of fit between the cultural and linguistic traits of these students and those of members of mainstream society. But as the research presented in this book demonstrates, "mismatch," "discontinuity," or "difference" are frequently inadequate terms for describing the language socialization experiences of Mexicano/Latino children in their homes and at school and/or for comparing these children's experiences with those of middle-class Anglo youngsters. By addressing continuities as well as discontinuities in language-use patterns, we move our analysis away from a strictly difference perspective and show how language use and language socialization practices in different settings and cultures may, under certain circumstances, converge. In later chapters, we enlarge upon this notion of cultural convergence to include descriptions of language-use practices that reflect Eastsiders' knowledge of multiple cultures and languages, including those of mainstream society.

In this chapter, we focus on data drawn from ethnographic case studies of language interaction patterns involving two preschool-aged, working-class, Mexican American children in home and school settings. As in most other ethnographic studies of language socialization, the main goal of the data collection phase was to gather language samples in "recurring and familiar contexts, interacting with those people with whom children are regularly involved" (Schieffelin and Ochs, 1986, p. 21). Pease-Alvarez identified and described the important recurring language interactions in which the two children participated in their homes and at school. Monthly recordings, lasting from three to five hours in each setting, yielded a total of 30 hours of language data per child over a five-month period.

To gain a richer understanding of what went on at school, Pease-Alvarez participated in classroom activities at the children's preschool, La Escuelita, working as a volunteer aide during nine months of field work. From the end of September to mid-December, she spent two to three days per week at La Escuelita, becoming familiar with the classroom routine as well as getting to know the three teachers, students, staff, and parents. Her participation in weekly staff meetings, parent-teacher conferences, and monthly parent meetings also helped Pease-Alvarez to better understand the pedagogical orientation of the program.

During this period Pease-Alvarez also spent time getting to know the families of the case study children, both of whom lived on the east side some distance from the preschool (see Figure 6). She visited the children at home weekly, and spent long periods of time conversing with their parents during her visits. She participated in important family events like baptisms, birthday parties, and baby showers. Like Shannon and Vásquez, she attempted to help family members understand how to deal with unfamiliar institutions and practices (e.g., filling out income tax forms,

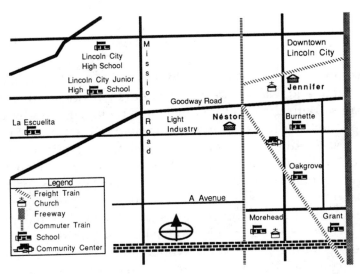

Figure 6. Map showing where Jennifer and Nestor live.

translating official letters and documents, seeking legal advice). In turn, Pease-Alvarez, who was pregnant during the study, frequently received useful advice from the parents about how to care for herself and her baby before and after childbirth.

From February to June, Pease-Alvarez recorded each child at home and at school once a month for three hours in each setting. Children were recorded during school between 8:30 and 11:30 a.m. (the duration of the school day) and after school, usually between 12:00 and 4:00 p.m. Although she observed and took on-site field notes during classroom recording sessions, Pease-Alvarez found that her presence during trial home recording sessions affected the way children and parents talked: Most of their talk was directed toward her. Because her goal was to describe the everyday language of the children and their parents, Pease-Alvarez decided not to attend the home recording sessions. Instead, she elicited information from the parents about what had transpired during each session immediately after the session was over.

THE CHILDREN AND THEIR
FAMILIES AT HOME

Like most of the Eastside children enrolled at La Escuelita, Jennifer and Néstor were the children of Mexican immigrants. With the exception of Jennifer's father, Gabriel Gómez, the children's parents immigrated to the United States as young adults. Gabriel was 13 when he first came to the U.S. with the rest of his family. After a year in an east side school, he returned to Mexico without his parents and finished two more years of schooling. At the age of 16 he returned to the United States and obtained employment as a cook. On a return visit to his home town in Mexico, he met his future wife, María, who agreed to leave her family and come to the United States, where they were married. After spending the first few years of her marriage at home taking care of Jennifer and later Gabrielito, Jennifer's baby brother, María obtained a part-time job working in a school cafeteria. During that time she also took ESL classes every morning at an adult education program located near her house. While she was away from home, Gabriel took care of the children. Both María and Gabriel were proud of the fact that they were able to care for their children without having to rely on babysitters. They did not approve of parents who left their children in the care of others for the majority of the day.

Arturo Hernández, Néstor's father, immigrated to this country from Zacatecas, Mexico, when he was in his late teens. He first settled in California's Salinas Valley and worked as a farm laborer. Like Gabriel Gómez, he met his wife Rosa during a trip to his home town. After they had married, the Hernándezes returned to central California. Arturo continued to work in the fields while Rosa occasionally worked as a daycare provider at a childcare center. After Néstor was born, Rosa quit her job. Due to the seasonal nature of Arturo's work and the strikes that frequently accompanied the ongoing labor disputes between farmworkers and growers, the family's income fluctuated from month to month. Dissatisfied with this instability, the family decided to move to the east side which they perceived as having more employment opportunities for Arturo. Shortly after moving, a relative helped Arturo find a full-time job with a tree pruning company that served companies and homes throughout the Bay Area.

Until Néstor entered La Escuelita, Rosa spent most of her time at home. For the first few years of Néstor's life, she never left her apartment without Arturo. After the family moved closer to the commercial sector of the community, however, she began taking Néstor for walks to the park and to stores. Unlike María Gómez, who knew how to drive and had access to a car, Rosa relied on Arturo to take her places after he got home from work or on weekends. By the time Néstor was four, Rosa supplemented the family income by babysitting for children in her home. During the study, she sometimes cared for a nine-month-old girl on weekday afternoons.

The Gómez and Hernández families' perspectives on child rearing differed, especially with regard to language development. When asked to describe the factors that contributed to Jennifer's language development, María and Gabriel focused on their daughter's intellectual abilities. They felt that Jennifer's success as a language learner, as well as her other early developmental accomplishments (e.g., toilet training, walking, riding a bike), were directly attributable to her intelligence. In contrast, Rosa emphasized what she did to support Néstor's language development. She provided labels for the objects in Néstor's immediate environment, talked with him about important events in his life, accompanied him most places, and never left him with babysitters. Unlike Gabriel and María, Rosa articulated the importance of her role in the language development process. She based her views about language socialization on her own observations of other children and their parents. As an observer of parents and children in Mexico and the United States, she had discovered that children learn best when parents make an effort to teach them using the kinds of strategies she did with Néstor.

Jennifer's free-spirited and gregarious nature transcended the boundaries of home and school and was often apparent in her conversations with adults and children in both settings. At home, she was the one who usually initiated conversations. For example, she routinely began meal-time conversations by asking her parents about their jobs or about events that had transpired while they were at work. Jennifer's comments about activities, objects, and people in her immediate environment often triggered conversations with adults, both at home and at school. Frequently, one of her companions' physical characteristics (e.g., a blemish, freckles, a growing waistline) prompted a question or comment from Jennifer that led to a longer exchange.

Néstor's school and home personae were quite different. At school he was quiet, almost reserved; at home he was a willing and enthusiastic conversationalist. Nearly every afternoon, Rosa initiated conversations with Néstor by asking him about people and events at school. Mother and son also participated in a conversational routine about the popsicles that they purchased from the *paletero* [ice cream vendor] who drove up and down most east side streets every weekday afternoon. During these conversations, Rosa and Néstor talked about the activity of the *paletero*, the quality of his wares, and, of course, the possibility of buying a *paleta*. They also spent time conversing as they played together, most often constructing elaborate scenes with Néstor's collection of miniature farm animals and soldiers. During these play sessions, Rosa often provided Néstor with labels and facts about the animals and people represented by the miniature figures.

THE CHILDREN AT SCHOOL

La Escuelita was founded 25 years ago by a group of Anglo mothers who were interested in providing a quality preschool experience for the growing number of Spanish-speaking families living in the east side. The school, initially staffed exclusively by Anglo volunteers was, according to its program literature, committed to the goals of "expanding the children's horizons and preparing them for school." A parent education component provided the children's mothers with weekly ESL classes, information about community services, and parenting classes. From La Escuelita's inception, children had access to instruction in both English and Spanish.

At the time of the study, La Escuelita was housed in a church located in a middle-class neighborhood of Lincoln City. It was staffed by two credentialed teachers and four teacher aides. Néstor and Jennifer attended the three-hour morning program which was taught by one credentialed teacher of Mexican and Italian descent and two Mexican-born teacher aides, both of whom were former parents in the program. The credentialed teacher, or head teacher, as she was called, learned Spanish as an adult, the two teacher aides were native Spanish speakers. Although parents and children used the title *maestra* [teacher] when referring to all three women, the head teacher was the one in control. It was she who most often led large-group instructional activities and who dealt with behavior problems. More importantly, her views about pedagogy were reflected in the school's official curriculum (i.e., in official verbal and written descriptions of the program that were made available to funding agencies and to parents).

The teachers' opinions about good nursery school instruction differed. The head teacher was an advocate of what she called a child-centered approach to instruction. She felt that teachers should provide children with a variety of meaningful experiences rather than engage in direct instruction focusing on skills. Consequently, when direct instruction did take place, it was done in the context of a larger activity, such as making a collage or weaving a placemat. Because the head teacher felt that play was the most appropriate context for learning, children spent much of the school day interacting with one another, playing with a wide assortment of games, toys, and manipulatives, and engaging in dramatic play (e.g., house, chase games, weddings).

In contrast, the two teacher aides felt that not enough time was set aside for direct instruction. They were strong supporters of the structured English as a Second Language and Spanish as a Second Language classes that the head teacher had eliminated from the program's curriculum. Both teacher aides also felt that an important part of their job was to focus on the affective aspect of their students' development. They were very affectionate with the children and spent time talking with them on an individual basis. Both aides also were viewed as important resources by the children's parents, who frequently sought their advice about child-rearing issues and, in the case of recent immigrants, about the community and country as well. On several occasions parents and community members have described the two teacher aides as *"el alma de la Escuelita"* ["the soul of La Escuelita"]. Many parents enrolled their children in the program because of these women's reputation as warm, caring, and approachable teachers.

Although the teachers' views about pedagogy varied, they all agreed on the importance of making sure that both English and Spanish were available to their students. The rationale underlying this commitment was motivated by two considerations. First, teachers wanted to make sure that their students would be able to communicate with teachers and other students. Because the majority of their students were monolingual Spanish speakers, this meant that teachers had to foster a learning environment where students felt comfortable using Spanish. Second, they wanted to provide children with some exposure to a second language so that they would feel comfortable when they encountered that language in kindergarten. Both considerations influenced the way the two languages were distributed at La Escuelita. To foster the acquisition of and familiarity with a second language, the teachers used an alternate-days approach of English one day and Spanish the next during circle time, which was the only time of the school day when all of the children were instructed as a group. The teachers also used visual cues and pantomine during circle time to facilitate children's comprehension when the language of the day was not their primary language. As they conversed with individual children during the rest of the school day, teachers based their language choices on their students' linguistic abilities, making it easier for the children to understand and be understood.

Like most of the other children of Mexican descent at La Escuelita, Jennifer and Néstor used mainly Spanish with their teachers, and their teachers responded in kind. Similarly, Jennifer and Néstor used mainly Spanish with the other children of Mexican descent at La Escuelita, even the few who were fluent in both languages. On a few occasions, they used English (usually one or two word utterances) with one of their three monolingual, English-speaking classmates. Because Jennifer tended to play with these classmates for sustained periods of time, she also participated in English conversations as a listener. In contrast, Néstor, who tended to play mostly with Spanish speakers, seldom interacted with English-speaking children. His contacts with these children usually lasted no more than a few seconds; and when they spoke, they did little more than exchange greetings.

Despite a common language and cultural heritage, Jennifer and Néstor had contrasting personalities and distinctly different styles of interaction, which were most striking at school. In fact, their teachers described them as polar opposites: Jennifer, the mischievous class socialite who was happiest in the company of others, and Néstor, the shy, almost contemplative witness of the many social events that occurred around him. Jennifer began each school day enthusiastically, skipping and chatting her way into the classroom. Once seated, she would recount an event, often something that had transpired on the school bus, to whomever would listen. She talked easily and at length with students and teachers as she participated in the full range of activities available to children at La Escuelita. An incessant stream of chatter and laughter accompanied her constant activity. Néstor, on the other hand, had difficulties adjusting to

La Escuelita. His mother Rosa accompanied him to school for the first month. They rode the school bus together and Rosa spent each day at school, usually no more than a few feet away from her son. On days when Néstor had to go to school unaccompanied, he cried. Elena, one of the aides, usually spent five or ten minutes hugging and reassuring him on those days. The crying episodes ended once Néstor had made two friends, Demis and Alejandro. Unlike Jennifer, Néstor seldom participated in the many small-group instructional activities that were available to students; nor did he spend much time conversing with his teachers. Frequently, teachers coaxed him away from his play with Demis and Alejandro in order to ensure his participation in special projects (e.g., making Mother's Day presents, decorating Valentine's cupcakes).

ADULT QUESTIONING STRATEGIES: SUPPORTING CHILDREN AS CONVERSATIONAL PARTNERS

Despite the differences in Néstor's and Jennifer's personalities, families, and language learning milieus, one adult questioning device, referred to here as a "contingent query," was used in both settings with each of the two children. When Jennifer and Néstor responded to their parents' or teachers' contingent queries, they either clarified or elaborated on a previous utterance. The three excerpts below contain examples of contingent queries that functioned as clarification requests. Such requests focus and maintain a child's attention on a previous utterance by eliciting a repetition, confirmation, or reformulation of that utterance.

> Jennifer: Esta va por Gabrielito (referring to a cookie).
> [This one is for Gabrielito.]
> María: ¿Cuál?   *Clarification request*
> [Which?]
> Jennifer: Esta.
> [This one.]

Jennifer: 'ama. La . . . la televisión no se dejan ver.
         [Mama. The television doesn't let them see.]
  María: ¿Cómo?   *Clarification request*
         [What?]
Jennifer: La televisión de nosotros no sirve.
         [Our television doesn't work.]

Jennifer: Este está malo (referring to food on her plate).
         [This is bad.]
  María: ¿Está malo?   *Clarification request*
         [It's bad?]
Jennifer: Sí.
         [Yes.]

Responses to the second type of contingent query, an elaboration request, provide new information about a child's previous utterance. Some responses develop propositions by specifying their underlying antecedent conditions (e.g., reasons, origins, previous events). In the following example, the adult's elaboration request elicited the reason underlying the child's previous proposition.

Néstor: Quiero uno de éstos (pointing to a magic marker).
         [I want one of these.]
  Rosa: ¿Dónde están los otros?   *Elaboration request*
         [Where are the others?]
Néstor: Yo no sé.
         [I don't know.]

Other elaboration requests elicit responses that provide information about the referent of a noun phrase. Responses to these requests include attributes, names, functions, evaluatory remarks or opinions, and definitions. In the following exchange, the child provides additional information about the doll she just mentioned.

Jennifer: Yo tengo una muñeca.
         [I have a doll.]
  Teacher: ¿Qué más puedes decir de la muñeca?   *Elaboration request*

[What else can you say about the doll?]
Jennifer: . . . Tiene un vestido.
[She has a dress.]

THE SIGNIFICANCE OF
CONTINGENT QUERIES

Researchers and theorists claim that both types of contingent queries contribute to children's oral language development. As turn-allocation devices, contingent queries simultaneously signal the child to take his or her conversational turn and contribute to an awareness that conversation is a jointly accomplished activity sustained by the verbal contributions of two or more participants. Children may also glean important information about the forms of the language they are acquiring from adults' contingent queries. For example, clarification requests that contain corrected forms of a child's utterance may represent an important source of linguistic data that children will eventually incorporate into their grammar. In the following exchange, Jennifer's teacher uses a contingent query that substitutes the more explicit verb *soñar* [to dream] for *pensar* [to think], the verb Jennifer had just used.

Jennifer: . . . Yo pensé que yo tenía una caja de juguetes.
    [I thought that I had a box of toys.]
Teacher: ¿Soñaste que tú tenías una caja de juguetes?
    [You dreamt that you had a box of toys?]
Jennifer: Sí.
    [Yes.]

The interactive aspect of exchanges containing contingent queries also plays an important role in children's language development. Brown (1968) has argued that adults' use of questions that contain partial repetitions of children's utterances provide information about grammar that cannot be easily derived from exposure to unconnected sentences. He states that the "changes produced in sentences as they move between persons in discourse may be the richest data for the discovery of grammar" (p. 288). Others impressed by the interactive aspect of this discourse device have described adult contingent queries as scaffolds or supports that children may initially need to enlarge and to fill out their own verbal contributions. Scollon (1979) has argued that young children's experiences with contingent queries in exchanges that he calls vertical constructions are the forerunners to longer, more syntactically complex constructions. For example, in the following exchanges (Scollon, 1979, p. 220–1), adults participate in these vertical constructions by using questions that appear to ask Brenda, a child just under the age of two, to complete or extend a previous utterance.

> Brenda: Kimby. [Kimby is a cousin who was not
> present – nor were any of her toys or other
> things. Thus there was no obvious meaning
> to utterance that could be inferred from the
> context.]
> Mother: What about Kimby?
> Child: Close. Hiding.
> Researcher: Hiding? What's hiding?
> Child: Balloon.

When describing these exchanges, Scollon states, "In both cases what can be seen is that the other speakers have taken Brenda's first utterances as the statement of a topic and have asked her to clarify it or comment on it." With time, Scollon observed Brenda providing both topic and comment within the same utterance, which led him to conclude that the development of topic-comment construction, at least for this child, may have originated in vertical constructions.[1]

Contingent queries have also been described as important aids to children's literacy development. In fact, in their later work investigating contexts for literacy development in mainstream and ethnic minority communities, the Scollons (1981) concluded that vertical constructions teach children to structure information in ways reminiscent of essayist literacy. Central to the structure underlying this style of literacy is the "creation of an explicit, grammatically and lexically marked information structure which is high in new information" (p. 90). Adults' elaboration requests provide children with the cues that let them know where and what kind of new information needs to be included in stretches of talk.

In discussing the relevance of oral language experiences for children's literacy development, Snow and Dickinson (1992) emphasize the importance of social interactions that help children develop their ability to produce and understand decontextualized language. At least two reasons underly this view. First, when children use decontextualized talk that, unlike most face-to-face verbal interactions, shares features of written language, they also become familiar with the language of written text. Second, when adults help children produce these stretches of talk through the use of devices like elaboration and clarification requests, they are also providing children with frameworks for understanding and producing the kind of language that they will later encounter as readers and writers.

Contingent queries are also reminiscent of the supports that successful readers and writers use. As Calkins (1986) has noted, children and adults query themselves about text as they read and write. Pease-Alvarez has observed teachers and older students who use contingent queries when reading with or to young children.[2] Their questions provide these new readers with opportunities to extend or clarify their oral reflections about a piece of writing. Contingent queries are also used in classroom writing conferences to help young writers elaborate, clarify, and reconsider their own writing. After reading a student's writing or listening to it being read out loud, teachers and/or other students participating in the writing conference use contingent queries to get the writer to clarify or add to what has been written. In addition to providing children with frameworks for extending and clarifying their verbal and written contributions, these early experiences with contingent queries in classroom settings may lead children to ask questions of texts as they read and write. Thus, this internalized use of contingent queries may represent a strategy for composition and comprehension that children draw upon when they read and write on their own.

Researchers interested in exploring the role of culture in the language socialization practices of minority and non-western populations claim that contingent queries and the two-party interactions in which they are contained reveal a specific cultural perspective on language socialization and child raising. For example, Ochs (1988) argues that this discourse device is an adult accommodation characteristic of middle-class Anglo-American mothers and middle-class European mothers, both of whom take an active part in their children's language socialization. Some researchers suggest that minority parents seldom use these kinds of accommodations because their views about child rearing differ from those of white middle-class parents:

> Studies which deeply explore the context of language socialization in family and community settings have shown that in some cultures, adults do not see infants of their community as conversational partners, nor do adults believe they have to teach directly or model speech for their children to learn to talk. (Heath, 1984, p.260)

Whatever the merits of these claims in other research, they are not sustained by Jennifer's and Néstor's experiences: Contingent queries were a recurring feature of adult talk with both children in their homes and at school. The next section examines the frequency and type of contingent queries used with each child in each setting. That analysis then provides the basis for reconsidering the cultural difference view as it applies to language socialization in Eastside.

DISTRIBUTION OF CONTINGENT QUERIES

Although both children had access to adult contingent queries in both settings, the frequency of these queries varied by setting and by child. As the data in Table 1 demonstrate, Néstor had access to more than five times as many contingent queries at home than at school. Jennifer had access to

Table 1. *Distribution of contingent queries for each child in each setting*

	Jennifer		Néstor	
Contingent query functions	School	Home	School	Home
Elaboration requests	63 (55%)	43 (43%)	12 (52%)	60 (46%)
Clarification requests	51 (45%)	56 (57%)	11 (48%)	71 (54%)
Total	114	99	23	131

similar amounts of contingent queries in both settings. Teachers used more elaboration requests than clarification requests with Jennifer and nearly equal numbers of each request type with Néstor. In the case of both children, Elena posed the greatest number of contingent queries (52 with Jennifer and 14 with Néstor). In the home setting, both children's mothers favored clarification requests, while Jennifer's father used more elaboration requests than clarification requests.[3]

There are several possible explanations for the distributional differences at school. Perhaps Jennifer's aggressive manner, humorous approach to interaction with teachers, and outgoing nature helped her gain access to teachers' queries. Néstor, who spent most of his free time playing with his best friends, may have been less interested in interacting with the teachers. The school's free-choice approach to instructional activities also may have contributed to the children's differential access to teachers. Jennifer often chose to pursue instructional activities led by teachers, whereas Néstor usually preferred peer play. Finally, teachers may have talked more with Jennifer because she was viewed as a more willing conversation partner than was Néstor.

CONTINGENT QUERIES IN THE HOME

At home, most conversations containing contingent queries were part of one-to-one interactions between parent and child. The majority of these queries occurred in the context of conversations about objects, people, or events that were tied to the participants' immediate time frame. For example, Jennifer's mother María often used contingent queries, especially clarification requests, when urging Jennifer to pick up her toys. In the following exchange, her clarification request *¿no lo va a llevar?* [You're not going to take it?] represents a departure from the rapid-fire commands she uses as she leads Jennifer through the task of picking up her room.

María: Necesito que te quites el cajoncillo. Eso no lo quiero ahí.
Jennifer: ¡Ay!
María: ¡Rápido! ¡Rápido! ¡Ahorita!
Jennifer: 'toy cansada. Ah, no, no, no, no. Estoy cansada.
María: Ah, pobrecita, ¿No lo va a llevar?
Jennifer: Estoy muy cansada.

María: I need you to pick up the little box. I don't want it there.
Jennifer: ¡Ay!
María: Fast! Fast! Right now!
Jennifer: I'm tired. Ah, no, no, no, no. I'm tired.
María: Ah, poor thing. You're not going to take it up?
Jennifer: I'm very tired.

Sometimes school-based knowledge was the topic of conversations containing contingent queries. For Néstor, this occurred most in the context of a routine exchange about his day at school. Rosa's use of contingent queries in these routines provided Néstor with the necessary cues for constructing a narrative account. These conversations, invariably conducted shortly after Néstor returned home from school, were always initiated by Rosa. For example, she begins the following conversation by asking Néstor who he sat with during lunch.

Mother: ¿Y Quién más estaba en tu mesa, hijo?
Néstor: ¿Maestra? ¿De maestra, mami?
Mother: No, de niños.

Néstor: Alejandro, Demis . . .
Mother: ¿Y quién más estaba en tu mesa, hijo?
Néstor: ¿Maestra? ¿De maestra, mami?
Mother: No, de niños.
Néstor: Alejandro, Demis, . . . este Fernando me dio un
      pedazo de tortilla.
Mother: ¿Sí?
Néstor: Sí. El lo que quiere ser mi amigo, mami.
Mother: ¿El lo quiere ser tu amigo?
Néstor: Uh huh.
Mother: ¿Y él te dio la tortilla para eso, mijo?
Néstor: Sí. Y luego dio un pedazo a Demis. Mira el pedazo.
      Ese vato se comió un pedazo grandote de taco.
Mother: ¿Y tú comías la tortilla que te dio?
Néstor: De taco. Demis se comió y luego dijo no quiero.
      Dijo, . . . "Te sirves tortilla entera." ¿Verdad, que
      sí?
Mother: Van a ser amigos, ¿verdad?
Néstor: Sí. Y también las niñas van a ser amigas todas.

Mother: Who else was at your table, son?
Néstor: ¿Teacher, of the teachers mami?
Mother: No, the children.
Néstor: Alejandro, Demis, . . . Fernando gave me a piece
      of tortilla.
Mother: Yes?
Néstor: Yes. He wants to be my friend, mami.
Mother: He wants to be your friend?
Néstor: Uh huh.
Mother: And he gave you a tortilla for that, son?
Néstor: Yes. And then he gave a piece to Demis. Look at
      that piece. That guy ate a big piece of taco.
Mother: And did you eat the tortilla that he gave you?
Néstor: Of taco. Demis ate it and then he said I don't want
      it. He said, . . . "Serve yourself a whole tortilla,"
      Really.
Mother: They're going to be friends, right?
Néstor: Yes. And the girls are all going to be friends.

In the preceding example, Néstor, with Rosa's help, describes the conversation with his friends. Rosa's questions help him provide more explicit information about the exchange and give details about the events at lunch and their consequences in a sequentially ordered narrative.

The audio-recorded conversations between Jennifer and her parents never referred to events at La Escuelita. However, Gabriel's tendency toward known-answer questions, a type of question favored by many teachers, may represent a way in which school or schooling influences ways of speaking in the home. For example, Gabriel uses contingent queries that resemble known-answer questions in the following exchange about a revolving globe that routinely appears during station breaks on a Spanish-language television channel. Jennifer initiates this exchange when she asks Gabriel a question abut the *"bola grande"* ["big ball"] that suddenly appears on the television.

TRANSCRIPTION	TRANSLATION
Jennifer: Una bola. ¿Por qué . . . está yendo una bola bien grande?	A ball. Why . . . is a big ball moving?
Gabriel: ¿Mmm?	Mmm?
Jennifer: 'stá yendo bola bien grande en ésa.	A big ball is revolving on that.
Gabriel: ¿Quién?	Who?
Jennifer: En esa bola.	On that ball.
Gabriel: Nosotros estamos ahí en esa bola?	Are we there on that ball?
Jennifer: Sí.	Yes.
Gabriel: Dónde. . .'ónde dónde está la bola?	Where . . . where, where is the ball?
Jennifer: Ay, toda la gente tiene una bola en su casa. Todos los lados. Y nosotros también.	All the people have a ball in their house. Everywhere. And we do, too.
Gabriel: ¿Y tú estabas viviendo en esta bola?	And were you living on this ball?

Jennifer:	Sí, toda la gente vive en esta bola.	Yes, all the people live on this ball.
Gabriel:	¿Quién dice?	Who says?
Jennifer:	Yo 'horita.	I do now.
Gabriel:	¿Por qué hizo así?	Why did it go like that?
Jennifer:	¿Qué dice en ésa?	What does it say in that?
Gabriel:	¿Cómo se llama esa bola?	What is the name of that ball?
Jennifer:	Telajamay. (nonsense word)	Telajamay. (nonsense word)
Gabriel:	¿Cómo se llama la bola ésa donde estamos nosotros?	What's the name of that ball where we are?
Jennifer:	No sé. Ey, triangle.	I don't know. Ey, triangle.
Gabriel:	Es tierra.	It's the Earth.
Jennifer:	No.	No.
Gabriel:	Esa bola se llama tierra.	That ball is called Earth.

Once Gabriel realizes what Jennifer is referring to when using the term *"una bola grande"* ["a big ball"], he uses contingent queries to test her knowledge about the earth and the way it is commonly represented as a revolving globe. In response to her errors and questions, Gabriel provides Jennifer with additional information about the globe. Although Jennifer's knowledge is not entirely adequate (e.g., she mistakenly responds that the earth is a triangle), she appears to realize that the revolving globe symbolizes the place where people live. Moreover, she generalizes the appearance of the globe on her television set to other settings when she states that everyone has a ball in their house.

This conversation, like all the others in her home that centered on the exchange of information, was initiated by Jennifer. In Néstor's home, by contrast, conversations about nonpresent events or entities were most often initiated by his mother. This difference may be attributable to differences in child-rearing practices that have a direct bearing on language socialization. Rosa, because she viewed herself as consciously involved in her child's language development, may have made a more deliberate effort to engage Néstor in conversation. Also, because Néstor was an only child, Rosa had more time available to devote to her son. Jennifer's parents, juggling the demands of two children, may not have had the time or energy to focus their conversational attention on their first-born, especially since they seem to have perceived her as being capable and ready to seek out her own linguistic opportunities. Thus, despite the fact that parents in both homes made use of contingent queries, they did so in different contexts and were motivated by different views about language socialization. This suggests the existence of important variations in the language learning milieus available to children from similar cultural and linguistic backgrounds.

Interestingly, features of each of the children's language milieus resemble characteristics described as present in mainstream homes and in some school settings. Rosa's use of contingent queries in collaboratively constructed narrative accounts is reminiscent of other school-based descriptions of the discourse used during sharing time (Michaels, 1981; Michaels and Collins, 1984). Gabriel's use of contingent queries to test Jennifer's knowledge of information mirrors the recitation scripts that have predominated in North American classrooms for the last century (Tharp and Gallimore, 1991). Although it is impossible to generalize this experience to other homes and settings, these findings suggest that the worlds of home and school, even for language minority children, may not always be clearly demarcated. Under certain conditions, or for certain groups, the language use patterns thought to be characteristic of just one setting may also be characteristic of others.

CONTINGENT QUERIES AT SCHOOL

Contingent queries at school occurred most often in the context of one-on-one or small-group interactions. Teachers sometimes used these questions as they helped Jennifer through an instructional task (e.g., story dictation, art project). This kind of scaffolding, so common in Néstor's home, did not characterize the teachers' interactions with Néstor because he seldom participated in these kinds of tasks.

Sharing time represented the one recurring instructional event when all the children at La Escuelita had access to adult contingent queries. Although the children chose an event or object to discuss in front of the entire class, sharing time was constrained by a fairly predictable structure, similar to the one described by Michaels. The head teacher routinely began this part of the day by calling on a child. The child responded with the name of an object he or she had brought from home or with a brief description of a past event. The teachers' subsequent elaboration requests focused on the object or event. When a child strayed from a topic or talked too long, the teacher usually ended the exchange or redirected the child's attention. For example, in the following episode, Jennifer's anecdote about her aunt and her doll (*"Mi tía ella echó agua a la teta. . . . Y dio leche a mi muñeca"* ["My aunt put water in the baby bottle. . . . And she gave milk to my doll"]) was cut short by her teacher's elaboration request for more information about the doll, rather than about events involving the doll.

Teacher: Jennifer.
Jennifer: Yo tengo una muñeca. Tengo una muñeca . . .
    [I have a doll. I have a doll.]
Teacher: ¿Qué más puede decir de la muñeca?
    [What else can you say about the doll?]
Jennifer: No más. Sí, tiene vestido.
    [Nothing else. Yes, she has a dress.]
Teacher: Oh. ¿Y qué hace la muñeca?
    [Oh. And what does the doll do?]
Jennifer: Se mea.
    [She pees.]
Teacher: Oh.
Jennifer: Sí. . . . Mi tía ella echó agua a la teta. . . . Y dio leche a mi muñeca.
    [Yes. . . . My aunt, she put water in the baby bottle. . . . And she gave milk to my doll.]

Teacher: Okay. ¿Jennifer, quién te . . . quién te la compró la
muñeca?
[Okay. Jennifer, who bought you the doll?]
Jennifer: Mi abuelito.
[My grandpa.]

Conversations about nonpresent referents (e.g., toys and
family members) were usually part of informal, spontaneous
interactions between children and teachers. Elena was the
classroom aide who most often used contingent queries to
pursue Néstor's and Jennifer's ideas during these interactions. Néstor initiated one of these interactions at lunch one
day by commenting on an impending war.[4]

Néstor: Van [hacer] guerra hoy. Sabes que van hacer una
bomba. Mira.
[They are going to make a war today. You know
that they are going to make a bomb. Look.]
Child #1: Va a explotar la bomba.
[A bomb is going to explode.]
Elena: ¿Va a explotar hoy?
[Is it going to explode today?]
Child #2: Sí.
[Yes.]
Néstor: ¿Verdad que sí?
[Isn't it so?]
Elena: ¿Quién dijo eso?
[Who said that?]
Néstor: Nadie.
[No one.]
Child #2: Ah, entonces leyeron en las noticias.
[Ah, then they read it in the news.]

The most interesting sequence in the database contains a
description of nonpresent entities and events. During this
conversation, Elena used 18 contingent queries to sustain
a dialogue with Jennifer that lasted more than 45 turns.
She began this sequence by asking Jennifer, who was pre-

tending to be asleep, if she was watching cartoons or dreaming while she slept.

TRANSCRIPTION	TRANSLATION
Elena: ¿Miraste cartoons cuando 'staba dormida allí, Jennifer?	Did you watch cartoons when you were asleep over there, Jennifer?
Jennifer: Mmm. Yo pensé que yo tenía una caja de juguetes.	Mmm. I thought that I had a box of toys.
Elena: ¿Soñaste que tú tenías una caja de juguetes?	You dreamt that you had a box of toys?
Jennifer: Yo, yo, que yo . . . trastecitos.	I, I that I . . . dishes.
Elena: Trastecitos.	Dishes.
Jennifer: Yo lo pensé y lo pensé que tenia una monstrua.	I thought and I thought that it had a monster.
Elena: ¿Una monstrua?	A monster?
Jennifer: Sí, de juguete.	Yes, a toy one.
Elena: ¿Y qué había de juguetes?	And what toys were there?
Jennifer: La, la ropita.	The, the clothes.
Elena: ¿Ropita para la muñeca?	Clothes for the doll?
Jennifer: Saturnina [referring to doll's name].	Saturnina [referring to doll's name].
Elena: Oh. ¿Y estabas contenta?	Oh. And were you happy?
Jennifer: Ey, ey no.	Ay, ay no.
Elena: No, no estabas contenta con . . .	No, no, you weren't happy with . . .
Jennifer: Sí, sí está. Sí, yo . . .	Yes, yes it is. Yes, I . . .
Elena: ¿Si estabas contenta cuando soñastes eso?	Yes, you were happy when you dreamt that?
Jennifer: Sí.	Yes.
Elena: ¿Sí?	Yes?
Jennifer: Sí. Yo me tenía esta muñeca.	Yes. I had this doll.

Elena: ¿Tenías esta muñeca?	You had this doll?
Jennifer: Uh huh.	Uh huh.
Elena: ¿Duerme contigo ella?	Does she sleep with you there?
Jennifer: No. Yo me duermo en la cama chiquitita.	No. I sleep in the little bed.
Elena: ¿En la cama chiquitita?	In the little bed?
Jennifer: Del niño.	The boy's.
Elena: ¿Y el niño, dónde durmió?	And the boy, where did he sleep?
Jennifer: Y Gabriel, Gabriel va a dormir en la hamaca. Y el de Gabriel hice vuelta.	And Gabriel, Gabriel is going to sleep in the hammock. And Gabiel's flipped over.
Elena: ¿La cama qué?	The bed what?
Jennifer: La cama hamaca.	The bed hammock.
Elena: Hamaca. ¿Qué cosa es una hamaca?	Hammock. What is a hammock?
Jennifer: Una hamaca donde se pasea.	A hammock where you swing.
Elena: Oh. Una hamaca donde se pasea.	Oh. A hammock where you swing.
Jennifer: Ya no me sirve uno. Me gusta que me pasea.	Now it doesn't work for me. I like to swing.
Elena: ¿Por qué?	Why?
Jennifer: Porque no . . . Hay de hay de Gabrielito . . .	Because . . . There is, there is Gabrielito's. . . .
Elena: Jennifer, ¿crees que soy muy grande para tener la hamaca o muy chiquita?	Jennifer, do you think I'm too big to have a hammock or too little?
Jennifer: Chiquitita.	Little.
Elena: Oh, ¿está chiquita la hamaca?	Oh, the hammock is little?
Jennifer: Si – no. Yo no me sirve.	Yes – no. It doesn't fit me.
Elena: Ay tu hamaca . . . (child interrupts)	Ay, your hammock . . .

71

The length of this conversation may be due, in part, to the extralinguistic context in which it was embedded. Both Elena and Jennifer were free to focus their undivided attention on this conversation because neither was involved in any other activity. Also, unlike the topically constrained talk that characterized some of their other conversations (e.g., at sharing time), they did not focus on a single topic. Instead, Elena and Jennifer were both responsible for initiating and pursuing a series of loosely related subtopics. For example, Elena got Jennifer to discuss her attitude toward her dream after she used several elaboration requests that resulted in Jennifer describing the object that she had dreamt about. Elena also followed Jennifer's lead when Jennifer moved the conversation away from a description of her dream to a description of her doll and later to a description of her sleeping arrangements at home. Elena's elaboration requests were consistently successful in helping Jennifer to pursue the new topics that she herself initiated.

IMPLICATIONS

Despite differences in the language learning environments available to Néstor and to Jennifer at home and at school, adults in both settings repeatedly asked the children to clarify and elaborate on their previous utterances. These requests for clarification and elaboration were occasions when adults assisted the children by providing them with cues that helped them extend, explicate, and repair their own verbal contributions. According to recent theories about learning and social interaction, linguistic and cognitive abilities originate in this kind of jointly constructed activity. The verbal interactions described here suggest that teachers may contribute to students' learning by making their classrooms places where adults and students frequently use contingent queries and other scaffolding strategies while cooperating on a particular activity. Following Rosa's and Elena's example, teachers interested in enhancing their students' language development could consciously use contingent queries to extend their conversations with children. To achieve this aim, they may find Elena's tactic of following Jennifer's conversational lead useful. Although this technique is likely not to result in a focused conversation, it appears to be a successful way to engage children in extended dialogue, which in turn would give them access to important information about the structures, uses, and organization of language.

The differences in each child's access to contingent queries across settings should remind educators that their students cannot be adequately judged solely by the way they act at school. Néstor, a lively conversationalist at home, was much less involved in adult-child interactions at school. Obviously any judgment of Néstor's language-use practices that are based exclusively on data from the school may provide an inadequate picture of his conversational abilities and the language milieu available to him at home.

RECONSIDERING THEORETICAL PERSPECTIVES ON LANGUAGE SOCIALIZATION THAT EMPHASIZE DIFFERENCES

The data presented here provide a basis for reconsidering the difference perspective as it applies to the area of language socialization. Jennifer and Néstor's language socialization experiences demonstrate that ethnic minority parents may be as actively and deliberately involved in their children's language development as are white middle-class parents. Jennifer and Néstor's parents' use of contingent queries is one way that they manifest this commitment. Rosa's description of her role in Néstor's language development, quoted at the beginning of this chapter, is further evidence that she is conscious of her own commitment to his language socialization. Although Jennifer's parents tended to attribute her developmental accomplishments to her superior intelligence, in their commitment to using Spanish at home, they also consciously shaped her language socialization milieu.

73

As part of a recent study, Pease-Alvarez interviewed over 60 Eastside parents about their perspectives on learning and using language.[5] Most claim that their decision to use Spanish with their children is one means that they employ to make sure that their children maintain Spanish. For some parents, this goal is intentionally furthered by insisting that their children use only Spanish when talking with them. Parents' responses to the question "How do children learn to talk?" may be summarized in two ways: those answers which emphasize the role of the child in language learning and those that emphasize the role of others. The later view is most often reflected in our conversations with parents. Like Jennifer's parents, those who emphasize the role of the child feel that the children's intelligence or predisposition for learning are essential for learning language. Mr. Ariel, a participant in the study, expresses these sentiments in the following excerpt from our interview:

Interviewer: ¿Por qué piensa que no les ha costado mucho trabajo a sus niños el aprendizaje del inglés?

Mr. Ariel: Será que son listos o yo no sé . . .

Interviewer: ¿Será la inteligencia?

Mr. Ariel: Es, um . . . tiene uno más dificultad, todo es más difícil para uno aprender otro idioma, uno de grande o de más edad que ellos. Ellos lo hablan más fácil aunque están pues chiquitos pues las palabras que hablan las hablan más fáciles.

Interviewer: ¿Y por qué será?

Mr. Ariel: Ahí eso por medio de . . . de diferencia de cultura. Y usted lo sabe que está de cierto el niño lo hable más fácil cualquier palabra se les pega más fácil y uno tiene más dificultad para hablar cualquier cosa. Ellos tienen más limpios sus sentidos. Cualquier cosa se les graba más fácil. . . . Sí es cierto que se le hace a uno todo más imposible para todo. . . . Sí es la memoria. . . . Aprender de memoria pues es difícil, ¿no? Tomo ya más tiempo. Tiene uno menos

> memoria. Todo se le graba menos y para ellos
> es más fácil tan chiquitos. Tienen más sabid-
> uría. Todo se les pega más fácil.

Interviewer: Why do you think that your children didn't
have trouble learning English?

Mr. Ariel: Could it be that they are smart, or I don't
know . . .

Interviewer: Could it be intelligence?

Mr. Ariel: One [as an adult] has more difficulties. It's
harder for an adult to learn another language
than for a child. They speak it easily even
though they are little. The words they use,
they speak more easily.

Interviewer: And why is that so?

Mr. Ariel: It's a difference of culture. You know that it's
true that a child speaks [English] more easily.
Every word stays with them more easily and
[an adult] has more difficulty saying
everything. They have cleaner senses. Everything sticks to them more easily. . . . Yes, it's
true that everything is more impossible for
adults. . . . Yes, it's the memory. . . . To learn
by memory is hard, no? I take more time [to
learn]. An adult has less memory. Things stick
less and for them [children] it is easier. They
have more wisdom/knowledge. Everything
sticks with them more easily.

Those who emphasize the role of others in the language
learning process most often talked about what they did to
help their children learn. Some explained how they relied on
modeling and repetition to teach their children language.
Mrs. Garrido describes this process in the following interview excerpt:

Nosotros los enseñamos. Cuando ellos empiecen hacer ruidos
con su boquita "ah, ah." Empezamos a decirles, "Maa, Maa." Y
que ellos nos miran a la boca. "Maa, Maa" . . . Entonces

cuando ellos aprenden decir "Maa, Maa," les decimos "Paa, Paa" y así eventualmente hasta que ellos empiecen. . . . Nosotros ayudamos a ellos.

We teach them when they start making noises with their tiny mouths, "ah, ah." We start to tell them, "Maa, Maa" . . . Then, when they learn how to say "Maa, Maa," we tell them "Paa, Paa" and so on until they eventually start. . . . We help them.

Mrs. Barraza, who also emphasized her role in the language learning process, told us that she begins to support her children's language when they are newborns. As she sees it, her efforts will also help her children develop other abilities (e.g., learning to crawl and to walk). However, unlike Mrs. Garrido, who focused on the role of direct instruction, Mrs. Barraza emphasized the role of conversation. As she notes in the following passage from our interview, she feels that the conversations that she has with her two-month old have helped the baby take on the role of conversational partner:

Esta niña no tiene más que dos meses y le platica uno y ella quiere platicar para atrás. Ella le hace barulla a contestar para atrás y a mí se me hace chiste porque estaba bien chiquita tenía como mes y medio y le platicaba uno y ella hasta se esforzaba porque quería platicar o sea que quería platicar. . . . Si se enseñan a hablar pronto se enseñan ellas a hacer todo más rápido porque ya saben comunicarse y sin embargo si son más tardías para hablar se tardan para todo. Para caminar porque como no saben si uno no les platica no les pone a hacer las cosas ellas. No se enseñan. Entonces necesita uno enseñar al niño a que platique a que se mantenga parado para que se amacise a que se enseñen a gatear y todo eso.

This girl isn't more than two-months old and when one talks to her, she wants to talk back. She makes noises at you to answer back. I think its funny because she is so little. She was about a month-and-a-half old and if someone spoke to her, she made faces as if she wanted to talk, she wanted to talk. . . . If they learn to talk early they learn to do everything more quickly because they know how to communicate, and if they take longer to talk they take longer at [learning] everything. [They take longer] to walk, because since they don't know, one [an adult] doesn't talk with them and doesn't make them do things on their own. They don't learn by themselves. So one needs to teach the child to talk with you, to stand alone so he can get strong, to learn to crawl and all those things.

As these excerpts indicate, many Eastside parents see themselves as responsible and deliberate participants in their children's language learning process. Like middle-class Anglo parents, some follow their children's lead and accommodate their speech to their children. Many claim to involve their children in language teaching exchanges that focus on a particular skill and that are reminiscent of the kind of direct instruction that goes on in schools. Most also recounted how they had provided experiences and obtained materials that they felt would lead to or enhance their children's language and literacy development (e.g., providing trips to the library, purchasing crayons and paper, reading aloud to their children, engaging a third party to tutor their children).

Thus far, we do not have a clear view of the sources of these views or to what degree they are manifested in practice. Perhaps parents' tendency to support and promote their children's language development is not linked directly to ethnicity. Traits that cross ethnic boundaries (e.g., class orientation, birth order, age, number of siblings) may provide a more complete explanation of the way talk is accomplished in the home and a fuller understanding of parents' views regarding language socialization. Research that addresses these issues in Eastside families' experiences should help augment and refine existing theories about how sociocultural factors contribute to the language learning experiences of Mexicano/Latino children.

With respect to home-school differences, existing studies that emphasize the lack of similarity between the language used in these two settings often imply that differences exist for entire groups of children. Findings from the present study suggest that home-school differences may vary for individual children, despite a shared ethnic affiliation. At school, Néstor had few opportunities to interact verbally with teachers; at home, he had many opportunities for dialogue with his mother. In contrast, Jennifer had many verbal interactions with teachers at school and had access to many contingent queries there, as well. The suggestion that home-school discontinuity can predict the success or failure of an entire cultural group is untenable, given the potential for individual differences like those observed between Jennifer and Néstor.

Although Néstor interacted with teachers less than Jennifer did, and consequently had access to fewer adult contingent queries, contingent queries were a feature of adult discourse in both home and school settings for these children. A number of factors could account for the apparent similarity in parents' and teachers' discourse. Like many preschool programs, La Escuelita is organized to encourage the kind of adult-child interaction that is more reminiscent of the home than the traditional primary school classroom. The ratio of teachers to students is much less (6 to 1 versus 28 to 1) and, in the case of La Escuelita, teachers have many opportunities to converse with children, something that decreases as the children progress through the school system. Interestingly, Elena, who among three teachers used the greatest number of contingent queries with Jennifer and Néstor, shared the same ethnic and cultural affiliation as these children.

Finally, research on home-school discontinuity in language minority settings is largely unidirectional, focusing on how children rely on home or community interaction patterns when at school. Educators and researchers seldom consider how schooling affects language use at home. This study has revealed ways in which children's experiences at school enter into their conversations at home. Events at school were routine topics of conversation between Néstor and Rosa. Gabriel's experiences with schools and schooling may have influenced his decision to use contingent queries and other question types as a means of testing Jennifer's knowledge or understanding of particular subject matter. Similarly, the teaching exchanges that other Eastside parents rely on may be grounded in their experiences with schooling.

Our research summarized in this chapter underscores the similarities in the language socialization practices that are available to children across cultures and settings. Why these similarities exist is open to speculation. For example, certain universal behaviors may account for similarities in the way people use language with children. Also, as we have mentioned, social traits (e.g., economic status, family size) that are shared across cultures may strongly influence individuals' language use patterns. Finally, occasions for cross-cultural contact may be particularly relevant in communities like Eastside: Situations where cultures and languages interact may lead to new patterns of language use for one of those cultures. Sometimes, these patterns are borrowed from one group by another, thereby leading to similarities in ways of talking. Other times, new patterns of language use emerge from these cross-cultural interactions or occasions of cultural convergence. The next two chapters explore this latter possibility by using a cross-cultural perspective to examine the ways in which Eastside's Mexicanos converse.

Chapter 4

Bilingual children crossing cultural borders

Becoming bilingual and bicultural is a natural part of growing up in the east side. Most Mexicano children experience
their preschool years immersed in a largely Mexicano cultural environment where Spanish predominates. Once in
school, they start learning English and gain enough knowledge of Anglo culture so that they are well on the road to
becoming bilingual and bicultural. This allows them to benefit from further exposure to English in everyday life and to
the cultures that exist outside of their homes and schools. As
they are exposed to the media, mainstream institutions, and
individuals from two or more cultures and communities,
Eastside children become increasingly bilingual and multicultural. Their eclectic knowledge and skills, in turn, contribute to the children's ability to act as valuable resources
for their families by helping them to negotiate an unfamiliar
language and culture. Paying the rent, enrolling children in
school, receiving health care, and applying for a job are occasions when Spanish-speaking adults routinely call upon
their bilingual children to help them communicate more effectively with English speakers and to better understand institutional culture.

Ironically, outsiders to the community frequently describe
the east side as a place where English is seldom used and
where residents have no interest in learning it. Terms they
use to describe the east side, including "Little Mexico" and

"El Barrio," are often intended to convey the sense of a community that is immune, if not resistant, to the influences of mainstream society. As evident in the writings and activities of Rosalie Porter (1990), Linda Chavez (1991), and other representatives of conservative organizations like U.S. English, this sentiment characterizes the views of many proponents of cultural assimilation who are attempting to influence public policy in the United States today. In contrast, our work with Eastside children and families has provided a picture of a community continually striving to make sense of their multicultural reality. Understanding both English and Anglo culture is fundamental to this process and often involves children who have become bilingual in the role of cultural broker or translator.

By examining two bilingual children's everyday use of English, we describe the range of cultural and linguistic resources available to Eastside children and analyze the ways they draw upon and use these resources. In addition, we show Eastside children actively involved in their own and others' learning as they negotiate multiple languages and cultures. The discussion begins with a description of a boy named Sal and his contact with English that illustrates how he draws upon multicultural knowledge sources. Sal's experiences help us see the extent to which a child in the east side has access to interactions where English predominates. We then focus on Leti, and her experience as an interpreter, a role familiar to many Eastside children. Translation events that involve bilingual children are examples of intercultural transactions, a term we use to identify occasions when individuals use multiple knowledge sources involving two or more cultures and languages to create meaning, negotiate a task, or to solve problems. The language-use practices of these two children provide insights into the complex cultural and linguistic milieu fostered by the types of interactions possible in their daily lives.

The descriptions we draw upon in this chapter are taken from an ethnographic study focusing on five preadolescent Eastside children's use of English (Shannon, 1987). This larger study examined the children's social networks and the opportunities they had for using English. Shannon interacted with the children and their families on a regular basis over the course of two years and audio-taped many of their conversations. Her findings show that the children used their second language for a variety of purposes outside of school.[1] Occasions that required Sal and Leti, for example, to speak English were frequent and involved complex uses of language that call upon higher order cognitive processes. Moreover, a careful examination of these occasions provides us with insights into the benefits of and processes involved in becoming bilingual and bicultural in a community like Eastside.

SAL AND LETI: EASTSIDE MEXICANO CHILDREN

Sal Pérez and Leti Macías were neighbors. Sal, his mother, and seven brothers and sisters shared a two-bedroom apartment located just across the street from Leti's house (see Figure 7). Leti lived with her parents, two brothers, a younger sister, and her grandfather. A total of three adults and four children lived in Leti's house.

Sal and Leti are fairly typical Eastside children with respect to family origin, economics, and language use. Thirteen-year-old Sal was born in the east side, but his family returned to Mexico shortly after his birth, and then moved back to the east side several years later. Leti, eleven years old, was born in Mexico and came to the east side with her family when she was four years old. Both sets of parents were born in Mexico and were from the rural agricultural areas of the central highlands of Mexico. Once they settled in the east side, both the Pérez and the Macías families did not move within or out of the east side before these children finished junior high school.

Both families were working class. Sal's mother worked at an assembly plant located a few miles from the east side dur-

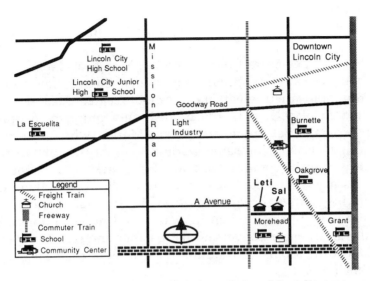

Figure 7. Map showing where Sal and Leti live.

ing the day and at a restaurant on Atlantic Avenue at night. Her three older children also worked and contributed to the household income. Leti's parents were both out of work; both had sustained work-related injuries. They supplemented their workers' compensation benefits by working odd jobs. For example, the Macías family and relatives who lived nearby often picked up free spoiled milk at a rural dairy. From the milk, they made cheese which the children sold door-to-door. Selling flowers at curbside stalls was another job that several of the Macías family members did occasionally.

The patterns of learning and using language observed in Leti's and Sal's homes were common among Mexicanos in Eastside: Bilingual children used both languages interchangeably, depending on the linguistic abilities of those around them. Generally, they used Spanish with the adults and preschool-aged children in their families; they spoke English with English speakers; and they conversed in both languages (often at the same time) with other bilinguals. Elementary-school-age children rarely spoke English at home with adult family members; as they grew older, however, they used more English with other bilingual children in their families.

Sal and Leti were first enrolled at Morehead Elementary school as kindergartners and remained at the school throughout their elementary school years. Sal's mother opted to place him in the English-only program in order to separate Sal from his sister, Marta, who, although younger, was in the same grade as Sal. At the time of the study, Sal was comfortable using both languages whenever necessary. He spoke Spanish at home with his mother and with his younger brothers and cousins. Outside his home he often used Spanish when he was called upon to translate. Sal was an eager conversational partner and frequently initiated discussions with adults regardless of their language proficiency.

Unlike Sal, Leti participated in the bilingual program at Morehead from kindergarten through third grade. By the time she reached fourth grade, she was deemed English proficient and, in line with school district policy, was assigned to a classroom where English was the sole language of instruction. Despite this shift in her schooling, Leti continued to use mostly Spanish at home with her parents and siblings and for a variety of activities that occupied her time outside of school. Moreover, unlike Sal, she wrote letters home to Mexico in Spanish and read from the family's Spanish prayer book and Bible as well as from the Spanish magazines and books she checked out of the local library. Although Leti was timid and tended not to initiate conversations with strangers, she was often called upon to translate for adult family members in unfamiliar situations.

Like Néstor and Jennifer, the children highlighted in Chapter 3, Sal and Leti had very different personalities and pursued different kinds of activities. The independent and gregarious Sal had many friends outside of his immediate family. He kept himself busy by bartering for bicycle and go-cart parts and by raising birds that he took from nests and later sold. He never hesitated to take a trip or to embark on an adventure. When he was in sixth grade, for instance, he skipped school and encouraged one of his younger brothers to do the same. They and two cousins took the bus to San Francisco for a tour of the town. Once in the city, they figured out how to get to Chinatown "by asking," according to Sal. When it was time to leave, Sal hailed a cab (as he had seen others doing) and instructed the driver to take them to the bus station.

In contrast, Leti stayed closer to home. She spent much of her time engaged in activities that involved her large extended family, most of whom lived nearby. For example, she attended Sunday soccer games, barbecues, and special celebrations (e.g., weddings, *quinceañeras*, baptisms, birthdays, anniversaries); and she participated in various family money-making endeavors, including cheesemaking, flower selling, and butchering. Being an older girl and a sister or cousin to preschoolers meant that Leti was regularly asked to care for younger children within the family network. At the time of Shannon's study, Leti was being groomed to inherit the role of family translator from her older brother Adán, who no longer had the time or interest to continue translating for older Spanish-speaking family members. Consequently, Leti's activities also came to include accompanying adults to stores, hospitals, doctors' offices, attorneys' offices, and places of employment.

SAL: A WINDOW INTO EASTSIDE'S KNOWLEDGE SOURCES

Although Eastside children are born into a world where Spanish and Mexican culture predominate, English and other cultures influence their lives on a daily basis. For many people of Mexicano/Latino descent, Spanish and Mexicano/Latino cultures tend to give way to English and other cultural orientations (e.g., Chicano culture). Survey data on the language preferences of Latino groups indicate that there is a rapid shift from Spanish to English occurring in many communities and that Spanish seldom lasts beyond the second or third generation (Veltman, 1988). Other researchers have documented the shift toward English in the language proficiencies and preferences of Latino children within generations (Wong-Fillmore, 1991).

Sánchez (1983) argues that the presence of a large concentration of Latinos is not sufficient to explain or predict Spanish and English use patterns. Rather, economic, historical, social, and political factors determine these patterns. Thus, while the east side is residentially segregated from surrounding neighborhoods, this does not prevent Mexicanos from having regular contact with Anglos. This interaction creates "dynamic bilingualism" among Mexican immigrants (Sánchez, 1983, p. 44), for they have access to a variety of linguistic and cultural resources that stem from their contact with different languages and cultures.

Preschoolers with older siblings may have a lot of experience with English but Eastside children are first introduced to sustained uses of English in school. As Pease-Alvarez (1993) has reported in a study investigating the language use practices of 64 Eastside children and their families, children who report using mostly Spanish with parents use mostly English or equal amounts of both languages with their teachers at school. Interestingly, many of these same children report using greater amounts of English with their siblings than with their parents.

Certainly for Sal, school provided a range of English-language contacts that contributed to his proficiency in English. One such contact was embodied in his special relationship with Mrs. Larson, who had been his third-grade teacher at Morehead. She continued to befriend him, and many other children, as they progressed through elementary school. During a period that was difficult for Sal at home, he lived with Mrs. Larson.[2] She helped keep him from dropping out of school during sixth grade by supporting his school activities and outside interests. With Mrs. Larson's encouragement, for example, Sal joined a Boy Scout troop and proudly wore his uniform for some school events despite his friends' jeering. For him, the advantages of scouting (especially fishing and camping trips) outweighed those of being popular with a particular group.

Because Mrs. Larson was a prominent figure in Sal's network, we examine her contributions to his repertoire of knowledge. With Mrs. Larson, Sal could discuss his dreams, plans, concerns, and ideas; he could also use Mrs. Larson as a resource for helping him to articulate his ideas and to achieve his goals. In the following conversation, Sal disclosed his plans for a science project at school to Mrs. Larson as they drove home from school.

> Sal: Hey, Mrs. Larson, do you know anybody that has, you know, little cars that go all around the track?
>
> Mrs. Larson: Remote control?
>
> Sal: No, just go around on the track. You know, just like that? You know anybody that has one that doesn't want it anymore?
>
> Mrs. Larson: Nah.
>
> Sal: It's 'cause I need a motor. And they have little, teeny, beeny motors.
>
> Mrs. Larson: What do you need a motor for?
>
> Sal: To make an airplane – my project for science. I'm gonna try to make an airplane. I volunteered to get the little motor.
>
> Mrs. Larson: For the group or for your . . . ?
>
> Sal: Huh?
>
> Mrs. Larson: For your group?
>
> Sal: For my project.
>
> Mrs. Larson: Okay. But you know who you might ask is Mr. Smith [a teacher at Morehead]. He likes . . .
>
> Sal: Oh, yeah. He took some of my motors away. They were little ones like this with magnets. And those work so good. You know I had one of those.

Mrs. Larson: And he took it away? Well, go to him and ask for it back.

Sal: Nah. I don't think he'll give it to me. I don't want one. Ask him if he has some big round ones. I don't want . . . he took away this flat one, this square, flat one, like this big. It was square, you know, and a round thing in the middle that turns around and it has magnets on the sides. That's what it is.

Mrs. Larson: Listen, Sal, I don't think he'd mind giving it to you if he had it. Usually, he's there at school. You want me to ask him tomorrow?

Sal: Uh huh. It's a little square motor. It has a round thing in the middle. It has two magnets. . . .

Mrs. Larson: Why don't you tonight draw me a picture and tomorrow at the meeting I'll ask him. Okay?

Sal: Tell him I have to build a glider, you know, with that motor. Make like a glider and put it on there.

Mrs. Larson: Okay, but you draw it for me. Look at all those rings on the street. Those dark rings.

Sal: Yeah . . . And you know I'll put a little battery, you know, those watch batteries. And you put thinner wire. What you do is just put thinner wire; it makes it lighter, you know – no plastic. And, um, the little battery and it turns (whrrrrrrr) and that's good. And then I could put a big propeller, about this big. And then you just make the frame, you know. Make the large wings. Make the back. Make something stand up, you know, make it real stiff. And just let it fly! Put some wheels on it and let it take off. You know, put wheels on it and it just. Even if it just runs, he [the science teacher] said, even if the airplane just runs, you got an 'A.' It just has to run. I don't know what you get if it flies. What do you think I'll get, Mrs. Larson?

Mrs. Larson: I don't know. If you put your mind to it . . .

> Sal: If it flies! What do you think I'll get?
> Mrs. Larson: I don't know anything about that stuff.

Clearly, Sal is a proficient English speaker who draws from multiple sources to accomplish tasks. For example, after Mrs. Larson reminds Sal that a teacher might have the motor that he wants, Sal uses Mrs. Larson, at her suggestion, to accomplish his goal. Further, the section of the conversation in which Sal details his plans for construction of the airplane demonstrates knowledge that Sal has acquired in his previous dealings with members of his social network. The vocabulary (e.g., magnets, glider, battery, propeller, frame) that Sal used suggests the wide-ranging nature of his experiences. On a hiking trip with Mrs. Larson a spirited discussion ensued among the hikers about the gliders that skimmed the peak which they were climbing. On a visit to a pet shop with Shannon, Sal had seen debris from a wrecked propeller airplane that was parked in a backyard behind the store. Sal's experiences help document some of the positive, nonrestrictive aspects of life in the east side. His world was not confined to people and situations associated only with the Spanish language and/or with Mexicano culture alone.

Sal's relationship with Mrs. Larson was characterized by the kinds of verbal interaction that many researchers feel contribute to oral language development. As a conversational partner, Mrs. Larson engaged in the kind of informal scaffolding referred to in Chapter 3. She extended and expanded upon Sal's verbal contributions and elicited clarifications and elaborations. She also provided Sal with very explicit information about English in the form of grammatical rules and word definitions. For example, in the following passage, she confirms Sal's correct formulation of the plural for "ox." (Note that this brief discussion of English grammar is embedded in a larger discussion of farming in Mexico.)

> Sal: You know, over there is Mexico, when you
> farm, right before you farm, you throw

> fertilizer on top and then you get these, um,
> oxes. They tie these oxes to some weird forma-
> tion, you know, that you can form any
> way . . . And we . . . And, you know, and
> leave something heavy on top so our whole
> family . . . We went on top of it, and my fa-
> ther, he just make – made – the oxes go . . .

Mrs. Larson: Oxen. Uh, huh.

Sal: Oxen. Oh, yeah. The oxen. I know about it.
Oxen . . . Go and, you know.

Mrs. Larson: You remember that, huh?

Sal: An ox is one and oxen is more than one.

Mrs. Larson: Right! That's one of those irregular ones.

Sal: Yeah. Oxen. And you know, I remember going
on top of it with . . . And, uh, it was fun!
Look at all the quail! Oh, my god! Look at all
those quails! Look at all! How many quails?
I'm gonna come quail hunting!

Mrs. Larson: (Laughs)

One thread in this conversation is the role that Mrs. Larson plays in Sal's acquisition of English and his shift into the
role of the learner. Mrs. Larson cautiously interrupted Sal's
discussion of farming techniques in Mexico to correct his use
of "oxes." Sal attended to her correction by suspending his
description and stating the rule for the plural form. This
kind of impromptu lesson is common in interactions with
second-language learners (Long, 1983; Schacter, 1986). It is
also reminiscent of the kind of correction and rule-stating
that mothers sometimes do with their children in their first
language. Sal's lesson additionally illustrates how ties to
Mexico (in this case family farming) supply knowledge that
Eastside children rely on during the course of their everyday
interactions.

Sal's verbal interactions not only provide us with a window into his socialization to and through language, they
also contribute to our understanding of the body of knowledge he had mastered and the way he chose to use his
knowledge. His contacts with Mrs. Larson offered Sal occa-

sions for drawing up existing knowledge sources to make sense of new, though not entirely unfamiliar, surroundings. The following excerpt, recorded while Mrs. Larson was driving Sal, Shannon, and nine other children to a nearby beach, was one such occasion.

> Sal: You know why they put that plastic there?
> Shannon: Why?
> Sal: 'Cause the water . . . The sun, you know, hits the water and the water goes up to the plastic and it gives those plants water.
> Shannon: I know another reason why they put the plastic. You know another reason why they put the plastic?
> Sal: Yeah. They get sun . . . reflects the sun to the bottom parts . . . And the plastic . . . there's water under the ground and the water goes up and when it evaporates it hits the plastic and stays there.
> Shannon: Right.
> Sal: That's what I meant in the first place.
> Shannon: Yeah. But I'm just saying that there's another reason, too. It cuts down on how many weeds grow.
> Sal: I know. And like in *The Voyage of the Mimi* [a book used in a classroom science unit] . . . They needed water and it was salt water, so they made one of those things, and then all that, you know, vapor hit the plastic and it started to run down into the pan. They did that to salt water.

As this example shows, Sal's knowledge comes from multiple sources. The hiking trip gave him the opportunity to travel out of the east side and exposed him (and the other children) to sights such as tomato fields, mountain peaks, forests, and animals not found on the streets of the east side. The trip also afforded Sal and the other children opportunities to talk about those sights. Sal's reference to the use of the plastic for evaporation described in *The Voyage of the Mimi* reveals a different knowledge source. The book was used in a fifth-grade science unit and was also the basis of an English-language television program. Sal retained such vocabulary as "reflects," "evaporates," and "vapor" from his exposure to the story. Furthermore, with the knowledge gained from *The Voyage of the Mimi*, Sal was able to confidently discuss alternative uses of plastic for water evaporation.

Eastside children's contact with English and their sources of knowledge are not limited to interactions with teachers or to school-based activities. Again, Sal's experiences are illustrative. His many hobbies and money-making ventures led to contacts with people with varied backgrounds. Owners and/or employees in many local businesses related to Sal's hobbies – pet shops, a magic store, an amusement park, a sporting goods outlet, and bicycle stores – knew Sal. He regularly inquired about things that interested him, and he was a ready explorer of the world around him. One of Sal's commercial endeavors, the renovation and sale of old bicycles, involved him in interactions with a variety of individuals, through whom he acquired equally varied knowledge. In the following conversation, Sal talks about his business contacts with a Vietnam veteran.

> Sal: I think he was, you know, a guy that tells . . . he leads the, the, uh, some of his troops. You know, he leads them where they're supposed to go.
>
> Shannon: A sergeant?
>
> Sal: Yeah. He was one of those, but in Vietnam. He has a lot of things. I think he has a Purple Heart. He says he killed a lot of men . . . and he has all this stuff. He has all these weapons. He has an M16. A good rifle and he has this other. It's like a rifle. It's about this long [holding his arms outstretched]. It's pretty weird and then it takes these big bullets, you know, about this big [extending his thumb and index finger] and they really . . . and you should see them. They're really sharp. And he has like a knife. It was, uh . . . the blade's about this wide and this long

> [dimensions like a machete]. It's pretty, you
> know, like it's pretty big. It's really sharp. You
> could use it as an axe.

Shannon: So you guys get stuff from him?

Sal: Yeah. He fixes sometimes our stuff when I can't
fix it. He fixes it. Like, see, I'm not that strong.
He charges too much for stuff and so I fix it my-
self.

Shannon: How long have you known this guy?

Sal: Long time. Since I was in kindergarten.

Children like Sal might be more likely to hear from their grandfathers about the exploits of Pancho Villa or Emiliano Zapata than about soldiers' experiences in U.S. foreign wars. Yet, Sal managed to make the contact with the veteran and to obtain a store of information from him. Although it could be argued that Sal is a special case and that he is unusually re-sourceful, from our perspective, the more important point is that the community of Eastside, and similar multicultural settings, offer children access to knowledge from a variety of sources. Thus, being of Mexican descent and living in a Mexican-immigrant community does not necessarily entail linguistic and cultural isolation.

The conversations reproduced in this chapter indicate that Sal was a highly successful second-language learner, that he had many and various opportunities to use his second lan-guage, and that he had multiple and varied sources of lin-guistic and cultural knowledge. One final example, which highlights Sal's bilingualism, illustrates how Mexicano chil-dren in the east side engage in social interaction in which they draw on their linguistic and cultural repertoires without consciously designating the interaction as Mexicano or An-glo, Spanish or English. The following exchange was re-corded as Sal and a classmate socialized on the school playground during recess (as shown in Figure 8). Sal had Shannon's tape recorder in his backpack and was boasting to the other boy about his mischievous recording at home the night before.

Figure 8. Sharing recording of television program.

TRANSCRIPTION	TRANSLATION
Jaime: You recorded it? In la house?	You recorded it? In the house?
Sal: Grabó la TV.	It recorded the TV.
Jaime: ¿Y estabas recording *Robotech?*	And were you recording *Robotech?*
Sal: Just a little bit.	Just a little bit.
Jaime: ¿Y grabaste las novelas y *Robotech,* huh?	And you recorded the soap operas and *Robotech,* huh?
Sal: ¿Cuál novela? Yo no grabé ninguna novela!	Which soap opera? I didn't record a single soap opera!
Jaime: ¿Oh no? ¿*Cristal?*	Oh no? *Cristal?*
Sal: Ehhh. Y tú la ves! Eh Jaime. None of your beeswax!	Ehhh. And you watch it! Eh, Jaime. None of your beeswax!

In addition to drawing from the two languages to compose their conversation, the boys also referred to two television programs: *Cristal*, a Spanish-language soap opera, and *Robotech*, an English-language cartoon. The boys' references reveal important cultural messages about the two programs. Jaime's accusation that Sal recorded *Cristal* is a playful taunt because this romance, commonly viewed by Latina housewives, is considered inappropriate for young males. The English-language *Robotech*, a militaristic cartoon that is a favorite of boys from a variety of cultural backgrounds, is considered the more appropriate program. Thus, this exchange reveals how the boys draw upon their knowledge of languages and culture as they construct a conversation which seems, on the surface, rather simple.

Overall, Sal's world was characterized by very little social and psychological distance from English and English speakers, making it what Schumann (1978) has termed a good second-language learning situation. Sal's strategies were successful in extending his social networks, thus providing him with greater opportunities to speak English, improve his English language skills, and expand his cultural perspectives. Sal learned not only how things are said in English, but also what is talked about in English. Furthermore, by combining his knowledge of English with Spanish and his understanding of one culture with that of the other, Sal maximized his ability to negotiate commercially as well as socially.

Mrs. Larson's contributions highlight the importance of interactions with native-English speakers. It is the quality of such interactions that makes them rich occasions for language use and development. The role that Mrs. Larson played is similar to that of the mothers and teachers discussed in the previous chapter. These interlocutors engaged in deliberate strategies to elicit the children's oral expressions. And although Mrs. Larson acted as a link to mainstream culture, she also provided nonjudgmental occasions for Eastside children to utilize their multiple sources of knowledge.

LETI: THE BILINGUAL CHILD
AS RESOURCE

The language broker is a vital resource in an immigrant community, and bilingual children frequently find themselves in this position when they are called upon to translate and interpret. Adult Mexicanos often have only a rudimentary grasp of English or primarily a receptive one. They thus require the services of intermediaries to help them transact their daily lives. Mexicano children, on the other hand, through exposure to English at school and in the larger society and through sustained use of Spanish at home, are bilingual, or nearly so, by the time they reach the age of ten. The bilingual child is "automatically" called upon to translate in situations where others are unable to communicate (Harris, 1977). In the east side, adults pressed their bilingual children into service as language brokers when a professional translator was not available. Research strongly suggests that the use of nonprofessional translators is prevalent among language-minority communities in this country and that translating is often done by children (Harris and Sherwood, 1978; Grosjean, 1982; Shannon, 1987).

Translation or interpretation events fit our definition of intercultural transactions because translating involves recourse to multiple sources of linguistic and cultural knowledge in order to create meaning, negotiate a task, or solve a problem. Bilingual individuals call upon their knowledge of two languages while interpreting utterances from one language into another and their knowledge of two or more cultures when conveying more than the literal meanings that underlie those utterances. A translation or interpretation event may represent an occasion when cultures as well as languages converge. Not all intercultural transactions involve translation, but all situations that involve translation are intercultural transactions.

The workers' compensation cases in which Mr. and Mrs.

Macías were involved created many occasions for intercultural transactions that required translation. There were daily telephone calls to lawyers' and doctors' offices, to their former places of employment, and to hospitals. Visits to these places often occurred weekly. Mrs. Macías usually asked one of her older children, Leti or Adán, to accompany her and act as a translator during her visits to a chiropractor.

The event that is the subject of the following transcription occurred after Leti's brother Adán entered junior high school and began refusing to accompany adults in his family to situations in which he was required to translate. With Adán's abdication of the role of the family's official interpreter, the part went to Leti, as the next oldest child. Mrs. Macías had been seeing a chiropractor frequently for a back injury that she had sustained at work, trying to move a 50-gallon container full of frozen food. In the office visit, Mrs. Macías was primarily concerned with letting her chiropractor know that she was seeing another doctor because she suspected that she had a separate problem in addition to her back pains. In the interaction, Leti translates for her mother (who is predominantly Spanish-speaking), and for the doctor (who is predominantly English-speaking). This encounter was one of Leti's first experiences as a translator. (Mrs. Macías had a tape recorder in her purse.)

Part One

TRANSLATION

TRANSCRIPTION

Chiropractor: (Entering the examination room and greeting Leti and her mother) Good, better? Terrific. Progress examination today.
Leti: Privacy?
Chiropractor: Progress exam.
Leti: Oh. (giggles)

Chiropractor: How do you feel about returning to work on the first of September?

Leti: First of September? That's when we're going to school?

Chiropractor: No. I want your mom to respond. How does she feel about returning to work?

Leti: Oh . . . ¿Que cómo se sentiría si va a trabajar el primero de septiembre?

How would you feel if you go to work the first of September?

Chiropractor: (Addressing Mrs. Macías as he begins the examination) A la derecha, por favor.

[Turn] to the right [side], please.

Mrs. Macías: Dile que yo no me siento bien pero si él quiere mandarme que . . .

Tell him that I don't feel well – but if he wants to send me that . . .

Leti: She doesn't feel well, but if you want to send her, it's okay with her.

Chiropractor: Well, we don't want to send her if she's not going to be able to work.

98

Leti:	(Silence)	
Mrs. Macías:	¿Qué dice, Leti?	What did he say, Leti?
Leti:	Que no la quiere mandar si no puede trabajar.	That he doesn't want to send you if you can't work.
Chiropractor:	But I would like to see her get back, and we'll work hard and fast in these next couple of weeks.	

According to Malakoff and Hakuta (1991), a translator such as Leti is faced with a fourfold problem: she must comprehend the vocabulary, comprehend the message, reformulate the message, and judge the reformulation's accuracy. At this stage, Leti had no problem with vocabulary or syntax in either language. Her job was further complicated, however, by the fact that she was required to carry out the four-fold problem in two directions: from English into Spanish and Spanish into English. This was no small feat. Dual-direction interpreting places a double burden on the translator and is an activity in which few professional translators engage (Thiery, 1978). The ideal direction, the one that is more likely to be successful, is into the translator's dominant language (Malakoff and Hakuta, 1991). Leti seemed to move through the four stages with relative ease and provided adequate translation in both languages.

Mrs. Macías and the chiropractor helped Leti by using translation prompts. For example, her mother asked, "What did he say, Leti?" It is not her level of familiarity with either of the two languages that hampers Leti. In fact, we see that she successfully translates from Spanish into English and English into Spanish. What she hasn't yet fully grasped is how to behave like a language broker. Her mother's prompts scaffold Leti's efforts and show how familiar Mrs. Macías is with a transaction that requires translation. Mrs. Macías understands some of what is being said in English – much as her chiropractor understands some of the Spanish. Rather than being a passive participant in the interaction, Mrs. Macías draws upon her own receptive knowledge of English and her familiarity with the basic requirements of a successful translation.

Part Two

TRANSCRIPTION	TRANSLATION
Chiropractor: (to Mrs. Macías) Sit down aquí.	Sit down here.
Mrs. Macías: Dile que estaba esperando Adán que viniera para que le explicará muchas cosas que le [unintelligible] que decir. Pero que te voy a decir a tí, para ver si tú puedes explicar bien.	Tell him that I was waiting for Adán to come so that he could explain many things that [unintelligible] to say. But I am going to tell you, to see if you can explain well.
Leti: (Hesitates)	
Mrs. Macías: Dile!	Tell him!
Leti: (Hesitates)	
Chiropractor: Something about waiting for . . .	
Leti: . . . My brother to come so he could explain some things, some things she wants to say.	
Chiropractor: Okay.	
Leti: But she's going to tell me.	
Chiropractor: Well, we'll talk about that on Monday.	

In this excerpt, Leti fails to convey her mother's message regarding Adán. Her hesitation galvanizes her mother into using an emphatic translation prompt. It is not until the doctor tried to figure out the dialogue for himself that Leti translates her mother's message. Even then, she is very hesitant. Leti's increasing selectivity in what she chooses to translate suggests that she may have begun to grasp the potential power that can be wielded by a language broker. Leti ends the segment by reformulating her mother's original message so that she, Leti, would appear in a more favorable light. Instead of her mother's message, that Adán's absence meant she would have to rely on Leti, Leti was able, by selecting portions of her mother's message and separating them, to convey to the doctor that in spite of Adán's absence, her mother would have Leti translate. The interaction appears to have afforded this otherwise shy and reticent child a measure of aggressiveness and attentiveness to her own needs by placing her briefly, in possession of more knowledge (i.e., that of two languages) than the adults had.

Leti's difficulty in acting as the translator for her mother was exacerbated by the nature of the situation itself. Miscommunication that occurs between doctors and patients is often due to the fact that the two parties do not speak the same language – even when they speak the same mother tongue (West, 1984). In the next part, communication breaks down when Leti does not know a word her mother uses.

Part Three

TRANSCRIPTION	TRANSLATION
Chiropractor: Let's go down to examination and I want to do a little progress exam.	
Mrs. Macías: Dile, mira, dile que yo me sinto muy mal	Tell him, look, tell him that I feel very bad right now, that I feel a lot, very bad. I don't

ahorita, que me siento mucho, muy mal. No sé . . . que ya no sé si es nada más de la es-palda porque me duele mucho el estómago. Estoy yendo al doctor y va hacer un examen para ver qué tengo en la matriz.

know . . . that I still don't know if it's just my back be-cause my stomach hurts a lot. I am going to the doctor to have an examination to see what I have [wrong with me] in my uterus.

Leti: She's, she's feel-ing, um, sick, a lot of sick . . . She doesn't know if it's her back or her stomach because she's going to another doctor because she's having trouble with her stomach.

Chiropractor: Who is the doctor?

Mrs. Macías: Con un doctor en Lincoln City . . .

With a doctor in Lincoln City, . . .

Dile que no me recuerdo cómo se llama el doctor.

Tell him that I don't remember the doctor's name.

Chiropractor: Well, that's okay. Good. Have him check her out and see what he has to say.

Mrs. Macías:	Dile que porque yo le dije a él que me dolía mucho aquí y él me dijo que tenía que ir con otro doctor y por eso yo hice otra cita con otro doctor y fui . . .	Tell him that because I told him that it hurts a lot here and he told me that I had to go to another doctor and that's why I made another appointment with another doctor and I went . . .
Leti:	¿Qué me dijo?	What did you say to me?
Mrs. Macías:	Que yo fui con un doctor a Lincoln City, con un doctor, un especialista de mujeres . . . Dile!	That I went to a doctor in Lincoln City, with a doctor, a specialist in women . . . Tell him!
Leti:	She went with another doctor in Lincoln City, a specialist in women.	
Chiropractor:	A gastroenterologist?	
Leti:	Uh huh.	
Chiropractor:	Good.	

Mrs. Macías interrupted the chiropractor's request that they move to the examination room because she wanted to give him more details on her health. The treatments that this chiropractor gave were for a back injury. Mrs. Macías had indicated to him at a previous appointment that she thought she might have other problems, and he had suggested that she consult another doctor about these concerns. She wanted him to know that she had made an appointment with a doctor in Lincoln City, but she also wished to reassure him that she did not intend to abandon his treatments for her back. This dimension of the translation is lost on Leti; she does not recognize that she needs to convey to the chiropractor her mother's intent as well as her mother's words.

The most serious miscommunication in this segment, however, occurred when Leti incorrectly translated the word *matriz* [uterus] as "stomach." Not knowing the meaning of *matriz*, or not knowing how to say it in English, Leti used an alternative strategy. Because her mother had just used the word "stomach," Leti used it. More confusion ensued when Leti correctly translated that her mother was seeing a "specialist in women." The chiropractor seems to have missed this new piece of information; he surmised that Mrs. Macías' problem was gastrointestinal, not gynecological and did not appreciate the significance of Leti's explanation that her mother was consulting a "specialist in women." The breakdown in this segment of the intercultural transaction is attributable largely to the adult speakers. Despite her unfamiliarity with the term "uterus," Leti competently surmised that the word has something to do with "stomach" and conveyed her understanding of the term by saying that her mother had visited "a specialist in women."

Part Four

TRANSCRIPTION	TRANSLATION
Mrs. Macías: . . . y dile que por eso que yo no sé si me duele mucho la espalda – dile que yo siento muy mal que hay días que tengo que estar todo el día acostada.	. . . and tell him that's why I don't know if my back hurts – tell him that I feel really bad and there are days when I lie down all day.
Leti: She's feeling sick from her back 'cause she's, all the time she has to be in bed.	

Figure 9. Bilingual child acting as the language broker.

Chiropractor:	Well, this is good that we get a second opinion from this person . . . Has she been? Or is she going to go?
Leti:	She's been there.
Chiropractor:	And what did he say?
Leti:	They're gonna see, they're gonna put some tubes into her stomach.
Chiropractor:	Okay. Can I get the name of him so I can correspond with him, talk to him?
Leti:	(to her mother): ¿Qué es el nombre de él?	What is his name?
Mrs. Macías:	No me recuerdo	I don't remember the doctor's name. . . . What?

	el nombre del doctor. . . . ¿Qué?	
Leti:	Que si tiene que tener el nombre de él.	He has to have that one's name.
Mrs. Macías:	¿Que él tiene que tener el nombre del doctor?	That he has to have the doctor's name?
Leti:	Quiere tener.	He wants to have.
Mrs. Macías:	Oh, dile que yo le digo el lunes.	Oh. Tell him that I will tell him on Monday.
Leti:	She'll bring it Monday.	
Mrs. Macías:	Porque yo no sé cómo se llama.	Because I don't know his name.
Chiropractor:	Let's go down to exam room . . . That's okay . . . Lunes [Monday] is fine . . . Let's go down to exam room. In just a minute I want to check your mom's range of motion and see if she's improved.	
Leti:	Okay.	

Leti translated the information about her mother's backache, but she left out her mother's concern again about seeing another doctor. For several turns, the chiropractor and Leti conversed without translating for Mrs. Macías and without the guidance of translation prompts. Leti responded directly to the chiropractor. Apparently using information she had acquired some other time, Leti even reported what the other doctor had proposed to do–"Put some tubes in her stomach."[3]

Despite the (largely pragmatic) problems that Leti encountered in this situation, she did move successfully between two languages. The encounter would not have been possible without her assistance. Given more practice, it is likely that Leti would become as proficient a language broker as her brother Adán. Because our data are cross-sectional rather than longitudinal, we cannot confirm the relationship between practice and proficiency. Adán's experiences, however, do provide some support for our speculation. At one point in their dealings with the workers' compensation lawyer's office, Mr. and Mrs. Macías decided that it would be best if Shannon translated for them. The lawyer's clerk found it frustrating to communicate with the Macíases through Adán because he doubted the ability of a twelve-year-old boy to understand technical details and to appreciate the importance of certain facts. However, when Shannon conducted the translation (by phone), she lacked the specialized knowledge which Adán had acquired by acting as a broker. Adán, present in the room, coached Shannon by clarifying points and providing critical details that Shannon lacked. By acting as the language broker, Adán had acquired specialized knowledge.

Translating provides bilingual children like Leti and Adán with the opportunity both to hone their language skills and to broaden their knowledge. Research on translation has shown a positive relationship between bilingualism and cognitive skills related to the acquisition and development of literacy (Bialystok and Ryan, 1985; Bialystok, 1986; Malakoff and Hakuta, 1991). Metalinguistic awareness – the ability to use language as a tool and to focus consciously on language – is one such ability or skill that can be realized through the knowledge and use of two languages (Malakoff, 1991). Bilingual children who regularly translate also learn about the underlying meanings conveyed through the use of language. Not only do they learn to convey meanings using two different modes of expression but they learn that some meanings defy a simple linguistic translation. Novice translators learn that they must draw upon extralinguistic information (e.g., cultural knowledge, situational cues) when conveying meanings across languages. Finally, translation provides children with new links in their social network which represent sources of knowledge seldom available to monolingual children. Acting as translator thus provides Leti, or any other bilingual Eastside child, with frequent, occasions for expanding her repertoire of knowledge and skills.

Children who regularly act as translators are much less likely to lose their ability in the languages they use as brokers because fluency in both languages is necessary for communication. Conversely, studies of bilingual children who were exposed to two or more languages from birth show that, once the child is in a language environment where one of the languages is not necessary for communication, his or her ability in that language atrophies.[4]

IMPLICATIONS

Contrary to the common misconception that linguistic and cultural isolation are prevalent in ethnic communities, Sal and Leti were not confined to a single realm of linguistic and cultural activity. Sal's wide-ranging social interactions in and outside of the east side contributed to his bilingualism and multiculturalism. In her role as family translator, Leti used her bilingualism and knowledge of two cultures to help others and, in so doing, she gained access to additional information about each language and culture. We also contend that children like Sal and Leti reap special benefits from participating in and negotiating their multiple worlds. Sal's ability to access a wide variety of linguistic and cultural knowledge leads to social and economic rewards as well as greater cultural and linguistic sophistication. Leti's role as cultural broker may contribute to her cognitive development by providing her with an occasion to treat language, and possibly culture, as abstract entities.

For these two children, being bilingual and bicultural and being part of a Mexican immigrant community like Eastside has its advantages. Yet, the bilingualism and multiculturalism manifest in children like Leti and Sal are resources that are ignored or systematically destroyed in this country. Although schools play an important role in introducing children to English and so-called mainstream culture, they seldom acknowledge children's native languages and cultures. When they do, the languages and cultures that are brought into the classroom may bear little similarity to those that are part of children's lives outside of school. Efforts such as bilingual and multicultural education may help reverse this state of affairs if children's native and second languages and cultures are given equal value throughout the curriculum and if moving between languages and cultures, a necessary and practical activity for those of us who live in multiple cultures, is also emphasized. For this to happen, schools should recognize and incorporate the multiple and varied modes of bilingual and multicultural activity practiced by students, their families, and members of their communities.

Chapter 5

Negotiating culture and language in the home

In the following transcription of a conversation recorded in February 1988, Rosa and Mrs. Neruda, her mother, help their friends Lorena and Tomás develop successful answers to questions posed on an application for amnesty under the 1986 Immigration Reform and Control Act (IRCA).

TRANSCRIPTION   TRANSLATION

TRANSCRIPTION	TRANSLATION
Rosa: ¿Cuándo le pongo que llegaron aquí?	When do I put you arrived here?
Lorena: Yo le puse desde del setenta y nueve.	I wrote from 1979.
Rosa: No.	No. (Arguing that they have been in the United States much longer.)
Lorena: Porque ella me dijo que no más del ochenta y dos. Y del ochenta y uno para aca porque si no me van a pedir todas esas pruebas.	Because she told me only from 1982. And, from 1981 to the present, otherwise they will ask for proof of that [of residence in the U.S.]. (She has conceded to go back three years more than required by law.)

Mrs. Neruda: Es lo que dice Doña Rosita. Dice, "Se van a chingar igual que yo." No hubiera dicho que estaba desde el 70 porque le pidieron toda la información de todos esos años para acá. Si uno nada mas necesita de cinco años para acá.

That is what Doña Rosa says. She said, "They are going to get screwed just like I did." She shouldn't have said from 1970 because they asked for the information for all those years. All one needs is only the last five years.

Rosa: Aquí dice, ". . ."

Here it says, ". . ." (reading letter)

Lorena: Porque ya . . . "Lorena Rojas, yo la he conocido, qué, desde . . .

Because already . . . I have known Lorena Rojas from . . .

Tomás: . . . del ochenta y uno.

. . . from 1981.

Mrs. Neruda: ¿Y sí tienen todo, todo del ochenta y uno?

And, you do have all [the documentation] from 1981?

In this chapter we focus on such conversations that prepare the members of four Eastside families to negotiate their needs in an unfamiliar culture and language. These conversations represent their own genre of intercultural transactions – one that exists at a more abstract level than the translation event described in Chapter 4. They are not face-to-face intercultural encounters involving members of different cultural groups, but rather goal-oriented conversations among friends and family members. These intracultural transactions focus on uncovering the tacit understandings connected to the second language and culture with the explicit purpose of providing a basis for effective action on the part of one or more members of the group. For example, one who is not familiar with the IRCA regulations would not know that to give an answer of a longer period of stay than required by law for amnesty eligibility would require them to provide additional documentation. Mexicanos, as the transcript suggests, have learned to respond within the intent of the law. To do otherwise, as Mrs. Neruda reports the case of Doña Rosita, will mean that "se van a chingar igual que yo" ["They are going to get screwed just like I did."]. Obtaining documentation was labor intensive, and Mexicanos were often unsuccessful as they had limited resources at their disposal to negotiate their particular needs with mainstream institutions.

The conversations of these Eastside families demonstrate how participants collectively learn ways of talking about and drawing upon knowledge and understandings that are outside of their individual experience. When confronted with unfamiliar knowledge and skills Eastsiders are socialized to seek the assistance of others to complement what they already know. In the previous conversation, for example, four individuals with varying degrees of information pool their resources to complete the amnesty application: Rosa's English skills, Lorena's personal history, Mrs. Neruda's knowledge of Doña Rosita's case, and Tomás' personal experience. The grace and skillfulness of this type of joint effort is particularly revealed in the way that Rosa, Lorena, and Tomás finish each other's sentences. When Rosa says, "Here it says," Lorena continues reading the passage, "Because already . . . I have known Lorena Rojas from . . ." which her husband Tomás finishes, "from 1981." Although Tomás is also asserting that Rosa write down 1981, he is bringing to bear his own personal experience and those of others as reported by Mrs. Neruda.

At work, in school, and in public life, Mexicanos of Eastside face situations which require them to negotiate the new culture and language. Even in their homes, where Spanish remains the language of communication, they are not completely insulated from the Anglo world. Regular reminders of the dominant culture come from many sources: the media, the daily experiences of family members, and the English-language labels on groceries and clothing. These encounters with the new language and culture featured prominently in many of the family conversations as family members relate their experiences or ask for assistance.

Nearly every aspect of Eastsiders' new social reality was revisited as family members talked during their leisure time. Sometimes the conversations were highly goal-oriented, sometimes not. At times, family members shared background information, contextual clues, and personal commentary as they "read" their social world – a segment of a television program, a photograph, a sign, or a wall hanging – were all described and discussed collectively (Vásquez, 1992). At other times, they were more interested in finding solutions to the difficulties that arise in intercultural communication. They described their interethnic encounters and related aspects of their unsuccessful or only partially successful interactions at the bank, school, clinic, or court. They wanted to know what had gone wrong, how they could have achieved better outcomes, and how best to prepare themselves *para la proxima* [for the next time]. Frequently, their conversations focused on forms written in English that one member or another had brought home to complete with the help of more knowledgeable individuals.

These everyday exchanges, which we term "Reconstructions," provide Eastside children with a basis for "reading" their social world and negotiating solutions to the problems posed by interethnic communication and social organization. The Reconstructions featured in this chapter illustrate how, in collaboration with those around them, children learn to interpret, explain, and debate the meanings and norms accompanying the information that enters their lives. In doing so, they simultaneously practice the same kind of analytic strategies that are the basis of standard literacy skills. As Freire and Macedo (1987) have pointed out, "Reading does not consist merely of decoding the written word or language; rather it is preceded by and intertwined with knowledge of the world" (p.29). That is, the interpretation of the written word is integrally connected to an understanding of and interaction with the broader social world. As demonstrated in Chapter 5, the broader social world of Eastsiders stretched far beyond the home language and culture. It included the languages and cultures of the community, school, and mainstream institutions.

In Eastsider's conversations, the boundaries between talk about oral and written texts blurred as individuals focused on the cultural and semantic underpinnings of interethnic communication. The overriding concerns of these conversations were the distribution of knowledge, interpretations, and decision making, regardless of whether individuals were talking about a written message in their possession or one codified elsewhere. Conversations sometimes centered on specific features of a text that no one had actually seen but one that was generally assumed to exist. An example of this is presented later in this chapter as a conversation regarding the rules of baptism. A close examination of conversations of this kind reveals that analytic strategies such as those labeled literate behaviors by Heath and Hoffman (1986) were common. In the 11 Reconstructions transcribed and analyzed for the study, the participants asked 109 questions requesting more information, indicating the collaborative nature of these interactions. On 68 occasions they used such analytic strategies as interpreting texts, saying what they mean, tying them to personal experience, and linking them to other texts. Also included were such literate behaviors that, Heath and Hoffman, note extend discussion on a single topic and lead speakers to explain and disagree with passages of text, make predictions based on it, hypothesize outcomes, and compare and evaluate texts or related situations.

The complex reasoning generally associated with print-based literacy activities practiced in schools clearly underlies the analytic strategies Eastside Mexicanos utilized in their everyday intercultural transactions. Defining what a particular aspect of language or culture does and does not mean is a literate activity; so, too, is rejecting, criticizing, and extending tacit propositions, whether the text consists of a segment of a television program, a gossiper's tale, an application form, or a sign on a door. Literate behaviors are not simply by-products of literacy. They are products of talking about knowledge in the social world, whether its form is written or oral (Langer, 1987). Among Eastsiders, oral skills, not print-based competency, provide the key to acquiring a literate use of language.

The following section sketches in a very general sense the social, economic, and linguistic backdrop to the specific form of interethnic communication that interests us here, Reconstructions. We describe two kinds of Reconstructions that exemplify how individuals in private conversations consciously and deliberately talk about a variety of texts. Finally, we discuss how the skills and knowledge base developed through Reconstructions fare vis-à-vis Anglo institutional culture, particularly in school settings.

LANGUAGE USE IN FAMILY SETTINGS

The language samples provided below were collected by Vásquez as part of an ethnographic study on the relationship between oral language and literacy in the everyday conversations of four Mexicano families (Vásquez, 1989; 1992). Having entered the community as a research assistant for the Stanford Interactive Reading and Writing Project (under the direction of Shirley Brice Heath) two years previously, Vásquez collected the language samples as an "unofficial" member of the Cristobal, Neruda, Orozco, and Zapata families. In 1988, as Figure 10 indicates, Vásquez lived within walking distance of the four families for seven months, participating in their intimate discussions, and audio- recorded occasions when family members talked about what they heard, saw, and did in the larger world of public and institutional Anglo culture. Over time, Vásquez collected many

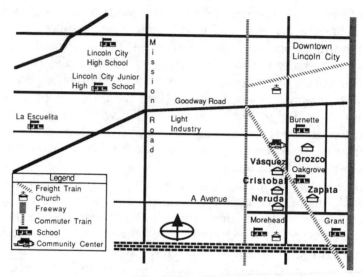

Figure 10. Map for the Cristobal, Neruda, Orozco, and Zapata families.

examples of Reconstructions, which were occasions when family members worked together to understand their worlds and used that understanding as the basis for effective action. These verbal encounters provided instances in which knowledge of the world both preceded and was interconnected with reading the written word much like Freire and Macedo suggest. This empirical evidence strengthens the case for a reconceptualization of literacy to include oral activities that expand conventional assumptions about the relationship between orality and written text.

This reconceptualization in turn, broadens the contexts for examining literate behaviors to include situations in which oral knowledge is preeminent: the everyday interactions of Mexicanos of Eastside. The analysis of language in both oral and written texts reveals the types and incidences of analytic strategies that are found in language patterns used specifically to talk about knowledge encountered in everyday situations. By comparing analytic strategies found in various texts, it is possible to arrive at generalizations about the effect of oral and written language on patterns of language use.

The Cristobal, Neruda, Orozco, and Zapata families share many characteristics with the other Mexicano families discussed in Chapters 3 and 4. All had lived on the east side of Lincoln City since they had immigrated to the United States and all had established elaborate social networks of exchange. Initially, the adults had joined a family member or *conocido* [acquaintance] who had preceded them to the east side. Thus, they acquired their hosts' network of friends and family. Although the four families did not belong to one another's immediate social networks, they knew of one another and of one another's personal histories. With the exception of Mr. Zapata, all of the adults came from the same highland region of central Mexico. The adult members of the four families had entered the United States without legal immigration papers, resettling on the east side where they found work and were able to raise their children. Most of the preadolescent children in the study had been born in the United States and thus were U.S. citizens. Several adults and teenagers were applying for amnesty under the IRCA plan, and others had already secured permanent residence status. The adults and teenage children in the Neruda family were applying for citizenship.

The families also shared characteristics with other Mexicano/Latino households throughout California and the United States (California Tomorrow, 1988). All were intact families and averaged 7 to 12 members to a family. In the Cristobal home, a friend or relative occasionally joined the family circle for indeterminate periods while looking for employment and/or other living arrangements. The other three families consisted primarily of nuclear family members for the entire three-year period Vásquez was in the community. All family members were relatively young; Mr. Orozco, at 53, was the oldest of the 38 members who made up the four families. The youngest child was a year old at the time of the study, and Mrs. Zapata was expecting her sixth child. With the exception of Mrs. Zapata, the adult males had been the first in the families to come to the area, returning to Mexico periodically until they were able to bring their wives and children and establish permanent roots in the area (McCarthy and Valdez Burciaga, 1985). As a teenager, Mrs. Zapata joined friends on the east side, hiring herself out as a housekeeper to a wealthy family in Concord. Periodically, she enrolled in English as a Second Language courses offered throughout the community but at the time of the study, she did not know how to read or write in English but could hold a very basic conversation.

The socioeconomic background of the four families was working class, both in Mexico and in the United States. All of the men had worked as laborers for the first few years in this country and the women as house or hotel maids. At the time of the study, Mr. Orozco worked as a machinist and was the only head of household to earn enough to allow his wife to stay home to care for their nine children. Mr. Zapata was a tree pruner; Mr. Neruda was an unemployed cook; and Mr. Cristobal worked as a cook at a restaurant where he had begun as a gardener 17 years earlier. The women had maintained their jobs as domestics. Their low literacy and language skills in English, coupled with their need to work short hours and temporary periods so that they could maintain the care of their home and children, prevented them from moving up the occupational ladder. The household expenses were often augmented by the wages of children who entered the work force as soon as they reached their teenage years. These young people held temporary jobs as store clerks, assemblers, food servers, or janitors. The Zapatas owned their own home; the other families rented their two-bedroom dwellings.

With the exception of Mr. Zapata, all of the adults had less than six years of schooling in Mexico, spoke little or no English, and had no schooling in the United States.[1] Mr. Zapata had the equivalent of a high school degree from Mexico and had studied English in a community college near Eastside.[2] All of the children in the four families were experiencing great difficulty in school except for Rosa Neruda. She was college-bound and went to France as a foreign exchange student during the course of Vásquez's study. The other teenagers seemed headed for departure from high school before completion or for completion with minimal academic skills. Most of the teenagers were enrolled in low academic tracks, received low academic grades, and were frequently truant. Their absence from school was often extended officially as a result of disciplinary action for truancy. The two older Cristobal boys and their teenage wives had dropped out of school before the study began; the two next-oldest siblings followed suit close to the end of the study.

Spanish was the first language for all members of the four families, including the children born in the United States.[3] These children remained monolingual Spanish speakers until they entered school. The adults had only enough basic survival skills in English to engage monolingual English speakers in a simple conversation. The older school-aged children were bilingual and were beginning to use more English in the home. Spanish, however, was still used to address adult family members. Although Spanish language and Mexican cultural values and socialization practices dominated in these homes, the effects of U.S. popular culture were evident in the choice of foods, music, dress styles, and entertainment activities, particularly among the younger generation. Like others in Eastside, the children in this study were beginning to adopt the cultural forms of their new society and to drop those preferred in their homes. They were beginning to watch more English-language television programs and were interacting with members of the opposite sex and older adults in ways that deviated from norms of the home culture. For example, these young people pleaded for more "freedom" to participate in activities separate from family-centered events. In particular, teenage girls, observing their peers date unescorted, asked their parents for the same privilege. Boys, on the other hand, began to challenge norms of dress and hair styles and chose to spend more of their free time with their peers.

Family members in all four homes had ample opportunity to interact with a variety of texts both written and oral. Information entered their homes through word-of-mouth, the media, and communiqués from many different institutions. Family members had access to letters, brochures, newspapers, children's homework assignments, and religious tracts; they communicated with relatives in Mexico through letters and telephone calls. Short, sometimes cryptic, printed messages permeated every aspect of their environment: For example, English labels and signs in their environment informed them about the clothes they were wearing, food they were eating, and direction they were traveling. Books such as novels and the Bible were also found in these homes. Mrs. Neruda, for example, realized that she could not help her children with homework assignments and so had bought them a three-volume reference book containing short summaries of key concepts in various academic fields.

As an unofficial member of these families, Vásquez spent countless hours in their homes, sleeping over, preparing meals, and casually socializing (see Figure 11). She audiotaped conversations in which family members talked about information and knowledge that entered their everyday lives. In some cases, children collected samples of family talk when Vásquez was not present. From these tapes 200 verbal exchanges that centered on multiple forms of texts embedded in job applications, verbal accounts of family history, television programs, photographs, or symbols were transcribed.[4] Of these transcriptions, only 74 which lasted over five turns and did not feature Vásquez as the main interlocutor were analyzed.

When analyzed, the transcripts yielded three patterns of language use in which members of the four families shared, expanded, and reinterpreted knowledge in their everyday lives. We have chosen to focus on Reconstructions here, although patterns labeled "Retellings" and "Extensions" also reflect how language and knowledge of either culture enters into the everyday conversations and how it is used to create

Figure 11. Making chepos.

meaningful interpretations of the social world. For example, in retellings of story-type texts, Mexicano cultural knowledge is shared as family history, contemporary events, gossip, and folklore. Extensions, collaborative encounters among several family members, build on knowledge and information from either culture that has entered the social world of the families. These kinds of family conversations are as likely to center on such events as the *telenovela* [Spanish-language soap opera] as on baseball games televised in English. Although, Retellings and Extensions draw on multiple knowledge sources to create meaningful interpretations of the world around family members, we focused on Reconstructions because they more adequately characterize the ways Mexicanos face problems posed by interethnic communication. In other words, Reconstructions more-readily reveal the intercultural transactions that individuals in this community engage in to create meaning, negotiate a task, or to solve problems. The following section shows the ways individuals in the privacy of their own homes focus on interpreting the meanings and expectations embedded in the new language and culture.

SOLVING PROBLEMS USING
MULTIPLE RESOURCES

Reconstructions typically averaged over 23 turns and involved a small, fluid group – of four to seven participants – that gathered in the crowded quarters of a given family's living room. Unlike much talk that took place in these homes, these interpretive sessions were focused, goal-oriented conversations that attempted to understand the meanings and nuances of a text. Typically, the family's most skillful member conducted the meaning-making exercise, posing questions to others, and then pooling their answers to form a collective reinterpretation of knowledge. Together, family members overcame their individual lack of familiarity with the English language and Anglo institutional culture. At the same time that these sessions reinforced cultural and linguistic resources, they also provided new ones that helped the petitioner meet the exigencies of the dominant English-speaking world. For example, the participants used Spanish to comprehend difficult vocabularies in English that would help them be successful in interethnic communication. Thus, the definitions of particular words or concepts, such as in the tax data Reconstruction on page 125 where Rosa asks how to say income tax, were often in Spanish – *intereses* [interests], *impuestos* [taxes]. In this way Spanish was an important tool in bridging the two cultures.

Reconstructions were a routine part of daily home-based interactions across the four families. The same scenario in which the television blared and younger children played noisily in the background while adults and older children grappled with the interpretation of texts was common in all four homes. A request for help, similar to Rosa's "*¿Cómo se dice . . .* [How do you say . . .] income tax?" in the transcript that follows called for participation in a problem-solving session. The requests-for-help set in motion a unique, goal-oriented dynamic among participants in the conversation. Unlike other family conversations, only adults or older children actively participated in Reconstructions. Younger children may have listened, but they remained on the periphery of the conversations until they were able to participate, usually until they became bilingual themselves and could contribute to the problem-solving. Although there were no overt cues, they clearly understood the seriousness of the discussion: They rarely asked questions about what was said and they tended not to interrupt the conversation with demands for attention.

Collectively, participants in these conversations sought to make clear the meanings embedded in a piece of writing and the strategies needed to maneuver through a bureaucracy. Those asking for help wanted to know what the text demanded. For example, they wanted to know what the letter from the insurance company stated, what a tax form asked for, or what was required for baptizing a child in the Catholic Church. They also wanted to know what was expected of them. They wanted to know how to conduct themselves effectively when faced with the procedural arrangements of large-scale institutions such as the Internal Revenue Service (IRS) and Immigration and Naturalization Service (INS), as well as local social and public services such as health clinics, recreation centers, the telephone company, and the employment office.

Two kinds of family conversations may be categorized as Reconstructions. One arises out of a need to respond to a printed form. The second emerges out of a need to understand institutional norms that are not always in written form and thus may not be readily accessible. In the latter case, the goal is to correct misguided assumptions about the finer details of contractual agreements, especially those associated with the medical profession, housing authorities, and legal offices. These decontextualized discussions may or may not involve explicit references to written texts, but it is clear that family members are trying to make sense of the procedural arrangements that characterize these types of institutions. We begin by examining the nature and function of print-based Reconstructions and then discuss the second, more abstract form.

"¿Qué dice aquí?" ["WHAT DOES IT SAY HERE?"]: SEEKING ASSISTANCE WITH WRITTEN TEXTS

Probably the most challenging texts the four families had to face were contained in the many forms distributed by such institutions as the medical profession, public utilities, and insurance companies. These jargon-filled, cryptic, and institutionally specific texts tend to frustrate native English speakers. For Eastside Mexicanos they posed formidable obstacles. Family members frequently asked one another for assistance in these cases. Mr. Orozco, for example, relied on his seventeen-year-old daughter to decipher the cryptic language of his medical bill so that he could determine whether he needed to make a payment. On another occasion, eighteen-year-old Rodrigo Cristobal asked his younger sister and his teenage wife to teach him to write a check. In addition to telling him where to place the amount in numbers and where to enter its equivalent in written form, his tutors also pointed out the function of "and" as a decimal point separating dollars and cents. Mrs. Zapata, a monolingual Spanish-speaker, turned to Vásquez for assistance in identifying documents which were not accounted for in an INS form. The elusive expectations embodied in such written documents as these elicited many Reconstructions in the four homes.

Nowhere were the texts more abstruse or more in need of interpretation than those related to government institutions. In the following fragment from a longer conversation, Rosa

Neruda finds the language of the Internal Revenue Service's SU 32 Tax Data Form more intractable than its functional uses. She knows that the form is used to regulate employees' payroll deductions, but she finds that its language defies translation. It is clear that she operates in contexts of limited resources. However, her bid for assistance in translating such words as "income tax" illustrates the way in which Spanish is reinforced in these situations, as well as how new knowledge is negotiated.

TRANSCRIPTION	TRANSLATION
Rosa: ¿Cómo se dice . . . income tax?	How do you say . . . income tax?
Older brother: Intereses.	Interests.
Mother: Impuestos.	Taxes.
Rosa: ¿Impuestos?	Taxes?
Vásquez: ¿Lo están haciendo en español?	Are you doing it in Spanish?
Rosa: No, I was just telling her what this form was . . . SU 32.	No, I was just telling her what this form was . . . SU 32.
Vásquez: ¿Ya le dieron el trabajo?	Did she already find a job?
Cousin: No, apenas voy [–]	No, not yet [–]
Rosa: She hasn't gone. Si te contratan, va a tener que llenar esto.	She hasn't gone. If they hire you, you will have to fill this out.
Cousin: Ah hah.	Ah hah.
Rosa: If they hire her, the employer knows where to sign here.	If they hire her, the employer knows where to sign here.
Vásquez: ¿En qué trabajo es?	What type of work is it?
Cousin: Es de janitor.	It's for janitor.
Vásquez: ¿Dónde?	Where?
Cousin: En Sunnyvale.	In Sunnyvale.
Vásquez: ¿En Sunnyvale? ¿Para usted?	In Sunnyvale? For you?
Cousin: Y para mi hermano.	And for my brother.

Vásquez:	¿Para los dos?	For the both of you?
Mother:	Ella es hija de un tío de mi esposo. No más que vivían en San José y se movieron aquí por la Main.	She is the daughter of my husband's uncle. They lived in San José and moved here close to Main Street.

As the designated family translator, seventeen-year-old Rosa negotiates the problems the difficult vocabulary poses by using others' knowledge of English and her personal experience. Her rejection of *intereses* [interests] and tentative acceptance of *¿impuestos?* [taxes] signals that she is not quite sure of the correct translation of "income tax" but is willing to make a decision weighing her own personal experience and the contributions of others. Through her interpretation of the language and intentions of the form, she will prepare the petitioner (in this case her cousin) for the eventual job interview.

In the previous Reconstruction, Rosa's immediate goal was to help her cousin fill out the tax form, but the broader goal was to position her cousin so that she could efficiently and effectively meet potential employers' expectations during job interviews. Rosa nears her dual goals in a later fragment of the conversation. She painstakingly arrives at two decisions (in italic and underlined): Her cousin can claim two dependents and she is not exempt from tax withholdings. Orchestrating a three-way conversation, Rosa moves from text to knowledge source to cousin and back again, weaving an elaborate web of meaning. She uses her personal knowledge of her cousin as building blocks to her final decision – her cousin is not exempt from withholdings this year because she did not owe any federal income tax last year, she is not a student, and she expects a refund this year.

TRANSCRIPTION

Rosa: (Reading text) "Total the number of allowances you are claiming. . ." *That means the dependents, right?* (interpreting)

Vásquez: *No, including yourself.* (explaining text)
Rosa: Including yourself:
  ¿Eres tu y tu niño, verdad? [It is you and your child, right?]
Cousin: Uh-huh.
Rosa: *¿No más?* (implicit decision reached) [That's all?]
Cousin: Uh-huh.
Rosa: (Reading text) "I claim exemption from withholding because this year I do not expect a full refund." Should we do that?
Vásquez: That . . . always.
Rosa: I hate that! I don't [–] (reacting to difficulty of text) *I think we should do that porque mira* [because look] (explaining) "last year I did not owe any Federal." (using text as support) . . . *She didn't work, she doesn't work, so she can't be that.* (evaluating and rejecting proposition in the text)
Vásquez: *So that's out.* (decision)
Rosa: *She can't be an exempt because she is not a full-time student.* (arguing with proposition)
Vásquez: *Right!* (decision)
Rosa: *It's got to be this year.* (explaining) (reading text) "I don't expect to owe any federal income tax and expect to have a right to a full refund."
Vásquez: I think that's right because she won't make the [–]
Rosa: *That's right,* 1987. (decision)

Step by step, Rosa manages the contributions of others, remaining generally tentative on the conclusions because of her own unfamiliarity with the technical language of the form. The session moves from the translation of English into Spanish to the interpretation of the underlying meanings of the printed form. Throughout the session the participants use a variety of analytic strategies to reach a consensus on the meanings and intentions of the text. When we use Heath and Hoffman's (1986) list of literate behaviors as a first step in examining ways in which individuals in these families talk about texts, we are able to identify those analytic strategies (in italic) that are most common across Reconstructions. These are: (1) interpreting – for example, "that means the dependents"; (2) explaining – for example, "It's got to be this year"; and (3) rejecting propositions – for example, "She can't be exempt because she is not a full-time student."

Extending the notion of literate behaviors also allows us to closely examine how decisions are reached in these conversations. Decision making involves an interactive, consensual process of consolidating information and finalizing opinions. Helping the conversants reach preliminary decisions allows the language broker to continue the process of meaning-making, moving toward the goal of preparing the petitioner to be effective in his or her intercultural transactions.

Although decisions are made at multiple levels and we cannot always identify at what point they are finalized, Reconstructions allow us to track the negotiations. The formation of a decision constitutes only one step in the problem-solving process. However, after a decision is reached, the information agreed upon is used again for immediate and future purposes. In this case, first as a written response on the tax data form, and then later, as part of the formalities of a job interview. The Telephone Bill Reconstruction that follows, the longest language sample (186 turns) in the data set, discloses more clearly the three-step, action-oriented nature of decisions reached in Reconstructions: formation of decision, immediate action, and anticipated action.

Although the conversation focuses primarily on the surface features of the written text – telephone numbers and names of cities, the lead interlocutor, Beto, pools the contributions of others, makes a decision, and then recommends further action. The following segment, one of 12 similar segments in this long Reconstruction, demonstrates the series of steps four members of the Neruda family and Vásquez take in establishing which calls were made by the family and which were mischarged by the telephone company.

TRANSCRIPTION	TRANSLATION
Mrs. Neruda: Pues ya les dije, "Fremont." ¿Qúe dice aquí? ¿"Newark," o cómo?	Well, I already told them, "Fremont." What does it say here? Newark or what?
Beto: A ver.	Let's see.
Vásquez: Yeah, Fremont, Newark.	Yeah, Fremont, Newark.
Mrs. Neruda: *Esto sí. Esto sí es de mi trabajo.*	This one is. This one is from my work.
Beto: *Okay, apúntelas. El treinta de noviembre.* (decision)	Okay, write them down. November 30th.
Mrs. Neruda: Pues sea como sea, pero éste es el teléfono donde trabajo.	Be that as it may, this is the phone number of where I work.
Beto: *Junte eso. Circúlelos y los manda par atrás diciendo que los que están circulados son las únicas llamadas de nosotros.* (decision)	Get them all together. Circle them and send them back telling them that the ones which are circled are the only calls we made.

In a single step, Mrs. Neruda reads the number and identifies its origin. As the conversation proceeds, a decision is reached to circle and write down the calls that were made by the family. Implicit in this interaction is the goal of not paying for calls on the bill that were not made by family members. But, first they must be able to isolate theirs from the ones incorrectly attributed to them: "*Junte eso. Circúlelos y los manda para atrás diciendo que los que están circulados son las únicas llamadas de nosotros.*" [Get them all together. Circle them and send them back, telling them that the ones which are circled are the only calls we made."] As Mrs.

Neruda confirms later in the conversation: *"No, yo ya les dije. Les dije, 'No vamos a pagar. Mándenos copias para saber.' ¡Qué casualidad que llegara el bill más que la última noticia"* ["No, I already told them. I told them, 'We are not paying. Send us copies of the bill so we can know.' Isn't it a coincidence that the bill reaches us only when it is the final notice?"]. Armed with the results of this extended negotiation, and after many calls and visits to the telephone office, 80 percent of the total charges were deducted from the family's telephone bill.

These print-based Reconstructions illustrate the literate activities that takes place in the everyday conversations of Mexicano families, activities, generally overlooked by researchers investigating literacy. Previous research typically has focused on the sociocultural characteristics of the home environment and literacy-mediated activities restricted to extended written prose. Other aspects of oral language activity that could be compatible with school-related literacy are not usually examined (Anderson and Stokes, 1984; Clark, 1984; Heath, 1980, 1986; Heath and Thomas, 1984; Hernández-Chávez and Curtis, 1984; Leichter, 1984; Schiefflelin and Cochran-Smith, 1984). Most investigators stress that these children's sociocultural environments determine their readiness for acquiring literacy and their speed at doing so. For example, some studies credit parents' experience with literacy and their level of schooling with fostering literacy skills and values (Clark, 1984; Hernández-Chávez and Curtis, 1984; Taylor, 1981). Other work has identified the process by which print is conceptualized. This body of literature helps us understand how a child learns to use written symbols. It does not, however, tell us how a child applies the knowledge learned from print, nor does it address the oral language background from which the conceptualization of print emerges. Although more research is needed to similarly pinpoint the origins of literate activity, Reconstructions strongly suggest that other "literate-type" oral language activities occurred regularly in the homes of the four Mexicano families.

When we focus on the second type of Reconstructions, we find that members of these families also had opportunities to use literate behaviors such as those listed by Heath and Hoffman (1986) around fluid and intangible forms of text. In a much looser structure with more tentative goals, family members nonetheless talked about "texts" with connections to literacy that were once removed from their social context, or that were vague or nonexistent. The text, in these cases, was held in the speaker's head and was recalled for the purpose of the conversation. These decontextualized discussions, not unlike those discussed in Chapter 3, attempted to make sense of such texts as a rental lease, a particular law, and the requirements for a Catholic baptism, all of which were codified elsewhere. Although the written forms of these texts could be found, the individuals had acquired information about them through word-of-mouth or the media. These experiences, like those around more tangible texts, gave family members many opportunities to use language as a tool for meaning-making. At the same time, they provided opportunities for family members to tie text to personal experience or link it to other texts; explain and reject passages of text; make predictions based on the texts; and compare and evaluate texts or related situations (Heath and Hoffman).

"*CÓMO SE HACE AQUÍ* . . . " ["HOW DO WE DO THAT HERE?"]: MAKING SENSE OF INSTITUTIONAL NORMS

Unlike print-based Reconstructions, those that occurred without print began serendipitously in the middle of conversations when a participant pointed out an inconsistency in someone's knowledge base. Although the absence of written text did not frame the conversation as a problem-solving activity, there was an implicit, if not immediate, goal; namely to prepare individuals for interethnic encounters. Once the problem was posed, the conversations continued in ways very much like those that occurred in print-based Reconstructions. A more knowledgeable individual took the lead and drew on the experience and knowledge of others to make sense of such things as institutional stipulations and procedural arrangements. The decisions reached, though much less substantive and often inconclusive, were nevertheless collectively constructed and literacy-related. That is, individuals used the analytic strategies of interpreting, explaining, and arguing with portions of an elusively referenced text, as well as forming decisions based on the contributions of others.

These conversations attempt to make sense of codified forms of texts which are frequently inaccessible for reasons of language, education, or literacy, yet pose very real problems for Mexicanos. If interpreting print-based texts strained a family's available resources, these texts represented an almost insurmountable challenge. Knowledge of English and its specialized uses, as well as knowledge of the operating principles of the particular institution placed Eastsiders in a much more vulnerable position. For example, during an extended conversation in the Neruda home about racial discrimination practiced by landlords, the group (composed of Vásquez, Mr. Neruda's mother, and his brothers José and Lorenzo) digressed on the subject of a rental lease, a text codified outside of the context of the conversation. By pointing out the extent of his legal obligations in relation to the lease, the other participants sought to enhance Lorenzo's bargaining power in the likelihood of a future transaction with a potential landlord.

TRANSCRIPTION	TRANSLATION
Lorenzo: Mira, aquí está otro caso fresquecito de Manuel Serrano. De mi cuñado. Que según tiene contrato por un año [–] ¿A poco yo voy a tener con-	Look, recently the same thing happened to my brother-in-law, Manuel Serrano. Supposedly, he had a year contract [–] There's no way I would have a contract that would force me to stay in the house. I just leave and do whatever I please and if they send me to court, they can do so because I can't pay

trato por estar a huevo ahí en la casa por no salirme? Yo me salgo y hago lo que yo quiera y si me mandan a corte, que me manden porque no tengo dinero con qué pagar la renta ya señores. No más yo pierdo mi depósito o me entro al mes. Si lo pueden poner en corte por unas cosas de esas.

the rent, sir. I will lose my deposit or I can just change to a monthly contract. These kinds of things can lead one to court.

José: ¿Tomó contrato por un año?

Did he sign a contract for a year?

Vásquez: ¿Tiene un lease?

Does he have a lease?

Lorenzo: Y . . . ¿Que por que quiere quedarse por un año? Le digo, "Pues cuñado si es no más de perder medio mes, pues yo me salgo."

And . . . Why would he want to stay for a year? I told him, "Well, brother-in-law, if I were to lose only half a month, I would get out."

Jose: Pues sí, porque va a perder nada más el depósito

Well yes, because he will only lose the deposit.

Lorenzo: ¡Claro!

Of course!

José: Pero, si tiene el contrato firmado, no puede.

But, if has signed a contract, he can't.

133

Vásquez:	No, pierde todo el año. Pierde todos los meses que le faltan.	No, he loses the entire year. He'll lose all the remaining months.
José:	Y debe pagar todo si tiene contrato firmado.	And, he has to pay all of it, if he has signed a contract.
Lorenzo:	Yo me salgo y ya.	I leave, and that's that.
Mrs. Neruda:	No, pues cuando firman, firman.	Well no, when you sign, you sign.
José:	Le vaya bien o le vaya mal, tiene que pagar.	If it goes good or bad, you have to pay.
Vásquez:	Pero con un lease se puede consequir a alguién que rente la casa y se pasa el lease a ellos. Y después se vence el año, ya pueden ellos hacer contrato propio.	But, when you have a lease you can get someone to rent the house and you can pass the lease to them. And, after a year they can get their own contract.
Mrs. Neruda:	Hmm hmm, que supla ahí.	Yes, someone to substitute there.
Vásquez:	Sí.	Yes.
José:	Y eso de rentar uno imagínese lo complicado que es.	Imagine how complicated it is to rent.

The *contrato* [contract] is a document no one in the group had seen, but all assumed that it existed and that it had legal force. Lorenzo's seemingly flippant comment, *"¿A poco yo voy a tener contrato por estar a huevo ahí en la casa por no salirme? Yo me salgo y hago lo que yo quiera y si me mandan a corte, que me*

manden porque no tengo dinero con qué pagar la renta ya señores.''
[There's no way I would have a contract that would force me
to stay in the house. I just leave and do whatever I please
and if they send me to court, they can do so because I can't
pay the rent, sir.], challenges the stipulation that he must remain in the home for the term of the lease, and gives others
an opportunity to specify the terms of the contract, explain
the repercussions of noncompliance, debate the outcome,
and suggest alternatives.

In the next example, the Reconstruction is also based on a
text codified elsewhere, but in this case the conversants have
very little knowledge or experience of the text. This conversation centers on seventeen-year-old Camilo Neruda's possible career in law enforcement. The Neruda children and
Vásquez attempt to reconstruct the contents and meanings
of the Miranda Law. Watching a policeman on television
"reading" the rights to a suspect, Camilo announces, "I
have to learn that, too. *Esa es* [That is] – ah, you have the
right to remain silent."

TRANSCRIPTION

Camilo: I have to learn that too. Esa es, "You have the
right to remain silent." (repeats)
Vásquez: ¿Cómo?
Camilo: | The right to remain silent.
Beto: |
Vásquez: Do you know what that's called?
Camilo: | No!
Beto: |
Vásquez: It's called the Miranda Law.
Camilo: You can always read it off. You have the right to
remain . . . silent. I do not wish to . . . if you
speak or ask.
Vásquez: What happens is that they are telling you your
rights . . . They have to tell you your rights before
they arrest you.
Camilo: You have the right to an attorney.
Vásquez: Yeah.

135

Camilo: Si no les dicen los rights, les puedes . . . llevar a corte. [If they don't say the rights to you, you can . . . take them to court]

Vásquez: Yeah, if they don't read you your rights you have a better chance of fighting the charges.

Beto: 'Cause you haven't been told your rights.

This conversation demonstrates yet another situation in which Mexicanos attempt to augment their knowledge of Anglo institutional culture. It is clear that the teenagers' everyday experience has taught them important knowledge about the power of those who have been disenfranchised; at least, they have seen this act replayed numerous times on television. However, their vague notions about their rights, expressed in a variety of Standard English used in American courts, places them in a precarious position vis-á-vis law enforcement officers (deLeón, 1990). Had they had a more knowledgeable source such as a lawyer, they might have come to a better understanding of the judicial, cultural, and linguistic significance of "You have the right to remain silent." These teenagers have yet to encounter the full text of the Miranda Law, let alone understand the cultural presuppositions embedded in its language. They are still unaware of the potential for power inherent in the legal protection, equalization of role relationships and specialized use of common terminology of this law (e.g., the meaning of "silent"). Their level of knowledge at the end of the Reconstruction does not grant them the full benefits of the law and barely meets the minimal academic standards of literacy. In other words, they are unable to speak about it to the full extent of its meaning. Although the conversation could serve as the basis for further learning, that is not likely since these teenagers have few additional sources to tap for legal information.

Access to knowledge affects the ability to participate actively, efficiently, and promptly in society at large. The Cristobals, for example, held numerous discussions over a period of several months in order to obtain the correct information about baptizing their six-month-old twins in a Catholic ceremony. The parents' inability to read or write in either English or Spanish required them to rely on others' knowledge and experience. Family tradition dictated who shared the cost of the food, baptismal paraphernalia, and entertainment, but Mr. and Mrs. Cristobal did not know what was required by the Church. In the excerpt from the Baptism Reconstruction that follows, the parents pieced together the Church's guidelines for baptizing children.

TRANSCRIPTION	TRANSLATION
Mrs. Cristobal: Que porque tienen que . . . dijo la abuela de Berta que como le iban a enseñar el sacramento a la niña si ellos no estaban casados. Que tenían que prepararse primero los papases.	Because they have to . . . Berta's grandmother asked *them how were they going to teach their child the sacrament if they weren't married. That the parents have to be trained [take classes] first.* (explaining)
Mr. Cristobal: *¿Solo por eso no pueden bautisar la chiquilla?*	That's the only reason they can't baptize the little girl? (arguing)
Mrs. Cristobal: *No, que hasta que se casen ellos, pues.* Que le dijo una hermana a la mamá de Berta que pregunten . . . que vayan ellos y pregunten a la iglesia. Que le pregunten a un padre a ver qué les dice.	*No, until they get married.* (explaining) A sister of Berta's mother told her to ask . . . For them to go to the church and ask. To ask a priest and see what he says.

| Mr. Cristobal: | *¿Lo que no se vale es alguien que no esté casado y lo lleve?* | What's no good then is for someone who is not married to do it [to stand up as godparents]? (interpreting) |
| Mrs. Cristobal: | *Yo sé. Así le dijo la mamá de Berta. Dijo, "yo sé que tienen que dárselos a una pareja que ya esté casada pues que no sean [–]* | I know. That's what Berta's mother said. *She said, "I know you have to give the child to a couple [select a couple as godparents] that is already married, that is not [–].* (decision) |

The Cristobal's come to know what is expected of them by the Catholic Church by using the knowledge of those who have participated in other baptisms. Although the process is slow and the information gleaned not without flaws, the parents learn that to be acceptable to the Church, their twins' godparents must attend baptismal classes and must be married in a Catholic ceremony, and further, that both of these prerequisites apply to them as well. Interestingly enough, both the godparents and the parents were able to skirt the requisites and baptize the children without attending classes or being legally married.

In both kinds of Reconstructions, members of the four families exploit the resources available to them. These sessions prepare them for more successful encounters with the language and norms of Anglo institutional culture. Access to finer levels of interpretation, however, is limited by their lack of English fluency, low level of education, and limited understanding of the norms of the dominant Anglo culture. Thus, although socialization processes provide these individuals with many opportunities to develop analytic strategies to cope with the demands of interethnic communication, these strategies often lead to limited rewards when put into practice. Most institutions are not prepared to help bridge the gaps in knowledge and language inherent in interethnic communication. Few institutions provide translation services, and fewer yet take the time to inform their clients about available options. And, although specialized knowledge and skills are not outside the curricular scope of the school, they are not easily accessible to Mexicano children, who typically occupy lower tracks where the academic content is watered-down, disjointed, and unchallenging (Moll and Diaz, 1987).

IMPLICATIONS: SEEKING KNOWLEDGE FROM A COMPROMISED POSITION

The burden of making an intercultural transaction successful typically falls on immigrants, not on the social institutions with which they must interact. Mexicanos are forced to make bids for services, employment, or civil rights using incomplete – and sometimes incorrect – information. This greatly compromises their bargaining power. Family members' lack of procedural and specialized knowledge and the institutions' failure to accommodate the needs of cultural and linguistic minorities often results in Mexicanos abandoning their bids for service. For example, when regular channels proved fruitless, the four families turned to folk healers, local mutual-aid organizations, and a variety of unlicensed private businesses to meet their medical, financial, or personal needs.[5] This reliance on social networks of support and on alternative institutions to fulfill their needs is thus a critical component of Eastsiders' problem-solving strategies.

The problem of a limited knowledge base goes beyond lack of second-language fluency and literacy to encompass the cultural norms governing the language of the text. Family members not only need to know how to speak and read English, they also need to know the options available to them. Although some choices are defined by their own cultural traditions, others, especially those embedded in institutional culture, are often elusive or unknown. In the Tax Form Reconstruction, Rosa's cousin is not offered all of the options implicit in the concept of "allowance." Neither of her knowledge sources (i.e., Rosa and Vásquez) understood the full extent of the meaning of "allowance" or "exemption," so they contributed very narrow interpretations of both these concepts. Their discussion about whether the cousin was exempt from tax withholdings, for example, was moot because, as a nonresident alien, it is not clear whether Rosa's cousin would qualify for the exemption. The cousin would have benefited from more expert advice, but none was available.[6]

The Miranda Law Reconstruction also highlights the precarious position from which some nonnative speakers of English negotiate their rights. The Neruda children have a vague notion of the protections afforded by this law, however, for these teenagers, the gap between knowledge and power is immense. For example, Camilo's declaration *"Si no les dicen los rights, les puedes llevar a corte . . ."* ["If they don't tell them the rights, you can take them to court. . ."] skips over the intention of the law to protect individual rights. Ignorance of *los rights* automatically precludes any litigation to preserve them.

Mexicanos often find themselves in subordinate positions in interethnic encounters. Deliberations such as the Rental Lease Reconstruction illustrate some of the inequalities posed by English and Anglo cultural knowledge. As José's comment reflects, *"Y eso de rentar uno, imagínese lo complicado que es"* ["Imagine how complicated it is to rent."]. Dealing with institutional culture is not an easy task for Mexicanos. The verbal interactions reproduced in this chapter reveal the range and variety of obstacles posed by the dominant culture. Even though José and Lorenzo have acquired important information about the norms and expectations governing the terms of a lease, they nevertheless require assistance to master the more sophisticated levels of interpretation which would grant them greater benefits in a rental contract. Lorenzo, for example, is unaware of the possible stipulations which would allow him to break the lease: He can petition to be released from the lease if it is for less than a year, if he recruits prospective renters, or if his dwelling ceases to become a refuge, information that Vásquez provided as part of the conversation.

Access to knowledge, especially access to specialized knowledge, then, is one of the most critical factors undercutting the bargaining position of Mexicanos. The social networks of immigrants rarely include individuals with the knowledge necessary to achieve finely graded levels of interpretation. Although Mexicanos use all the resources at their disposal to meet the demands of immigrant life, schools could and should play a much greater role in facilitating their active participation at every level of society. The classroom, and specifically literacy training is an appropriate vehicle for the transmission of specialized knowledge and skills for functioning successfully in this society, but our conceptions of literacy must be changed dramatically. We must view literacy practices in a much broader context – one that brings into focus the oral language practices and available knowledge sources that make up the very foundation of literacy. In so doing, we will be able to acknowledge and build upon the varied cultural and linguistic resources that children from diverse backgrounds bring to the learning setting.

Chapter 6

Moving toward a recognition perspective

Some of the abilities and experiences of Mexicanos from the community of Eastside described in previous chapters are grounded in uniquely Mexican patterns of knowing and interacting. Some ways of using and thinking about language, however, are shared across cultures, and some are shaped by the users' experience of living and working in multiple cultures. Children and parents are key players in one another's language socialization. Parents perceive themselves to be deliberate and central participants in their children's language development, but children, too, are responsible for helping adults negotiate transactions with outside institutions. Thus, language socialization is a mutual endeavor, with adults and children sharing responsibility as they negotiate language and culture.

Language socialization among Eastsiders is rife with developmental opportunities. The everyday conversations that involve Nestor and Jennifer with their adult conversation partners provide them with knowledge and skills that they can draw upon as they learn about the details of their language and the modes of discourse that they will later encounter as readers and writers. Through encounters with English, children learn to talk about a wide range of information beyond that found in the east side. They extend and further develop their bilingualism and multiculturalism through intercultural transactions that require them to draw upon their languages and cultures to negotiate meaning. Moreover, the intellectual feats involved in these events entail the use of sophisticated cognitive processes that enable children to maneuver successfully in and out of a variety of linguistic domains. A case in point is the child interpreter who simultaneously operates in several mental frames as she or he facilitates cross-language communication. Linguistic capabilities often place children in positions of power as they advocate for adults in the family's social network vis-à-vis mainstream institutions.

LANGUAGE MINORITY STUDENTS AT SCHOOL

What happens when the school bell rings and language-minority children like those we have described enter the world of the classroom? To answer this question, we must first consider an important goal of schooling: enhancing the possibility for future social and economic security and advancement by preparing children to participate successfully in the world that lies beyond their doorstep, neighborhood, and local community, a world managed and controlled by nonminority groups. Indeed, school administrators and teachers see their job as one of preparing language-minority children for entry into the economic, political, and social sectors by ensuring that these children acquire certain skills and characteristics that will "guarantee success." Such efforts concentrate specifically on those skills that minority students are thought to be lacking – proficiency in English and an inventory of knowledge and behaviors found in white, middle-class society. According to Moll (1992) and others, the acquisition of English stands out as the factor that receives the greatest emphasis in the schooling of language-minority students, so much so that it usually overshadows other educational goals.

The overemphasis on English tends to detract from the quality of schooling many language-minority children receive. Students who are classified as having limited English proficiency are often thought to be deficient in other language areas. They are often relegated to a remedial instructional program focusing on the acquisition of basic skills and facts that supposedly match their English-proficiency level. Ironically, instruction in these programs often focuses on abilities that children may have already mastered in their native languages (Moll and Díaz, 1987). And if these students are poor or working-class, as is often the case, and consequently deemed to be from linguistically and cognitively deficient home environments, it is even more likely that they will have little access to instructional activities designed to be cognitively demanding. Instead, their instruction is likely to focus on artificial and text-based exercises that are removed from any meaningful or familiar context.

When we look at the way language is used in classrooms, we have further cause for concern. Despite the recent visibility of theories that call for increased verbal interaction among students in classroom settings, teachers of minority students continue to do most of the talking. Student opportunities to talk most often occur within the context of the recitation script – a teacher-dominated discourse sequence that bears little resemblance to the modes of talk that prevail in students' homes and communities (Goodlad, 1984; Ramírez, 1991). Teachers initiate this discourse sequence either by lecturing or by having students produce or read a written text that eventually becomes the basis for a series of questions that test students' knowledge of facts or skills (e.g., Mehan, 1979; Tharp and Gallimore, 1989). In most cases, teachers follow up students' responses with a short evaluative comment or another test question. This imbalance between the discourse of teacher and student is even more pronounced at the secondary level, where students are enrolled in classes in which teachers lecture and student participation is limited to quiet and furious note-taking.

Even well-intended teachers convinced of the merits of innovative approaches to discussion rely on recitation. For example, in our observations of east side classrooms, we noted occasions when recitation crept into learning events that were intended to provide students with alternative ways of using language. The following conversation between a fifth-grade teacher and her bilingual students occurred after the teacher participated in a two-day workshop on how to involve students in discussions of children's literature. In the workshop, teachers were introduced to the idea of limiting their involvement in discussions and of posing open-ended questions that did not require a single, correct response from students. Although the fifth-grade teacher found this approach intriguing, she had a hard time actually using it with students she considered to be weak readers. As the following excerpt illustrates, she continued to direct and control the flow of the discourse as she fired known-answer questions at her weak-reader group:

Teacher: So, who can tell me what the book's about?
Student 1: Johnny Appleseed.
Teacher: Okay. Who was Johnny Appleseed?
Student 2: About a – a kid who went around planting apple seeds.
Teacher: Planting apple seeds. Where did he plant 'em?
Student 2: All over the world.
Teacher: All over the world – or what . . .
Student 3: All over the country.
Student 4: Yeah.
Teacher: What country is that?
Student 3: Massachusetts.
Teacher: Okay. And where else?
Student 4: Ohio.
Student 3: Ohio.
Student 4: Indiana.
Teacher: All over the United States, huh? Okay. . . . How is it that he got to be called Johnny Appleseed?
Student 3: 'Cause he's . . .
Student 2: He was a real man.[1]

In addition to the prevalence of this discourse pattern in many classrooms serving language-minority children, these children tend to have less experience with certain modes of discourse than do their white middle-class counterparts. When children rely on language-use patterns at school that are unfamiliar to teachers, and vice versa, difficulties may arise that lead to negative judgments about minority students. For example, Michaels and Collins (1984) describe how one white first-grade teacher responded differently to the narratives black versus white children offered during a classroom activity called "sharing time." When responding to white children's narratives, this teacher was able to use questions and comments that helped the children elaborate on the topic of their narrative. In contrast, she was unable to successfully scaffold the verbal contributions of black children who produced sharing-time narratives that touched upon a series of related topics, rather than keeping to a single theme. When describing the performance of black students, she criticized them as "talking off the top of their heads, thinking up things to say as they go along" (p. 229). Even teachers who share the students' cultural and linguistic background treat children differentially according to their judgment of children's use of language. Maldonado-Guzman(1980), for example, found that Puerto Rican teachers on an exchange program in the United States tended to censor children who did not speak standard English or standard Spanish and did not conform to their particular cultural views and ideals. Maldonado-Guzman goes on to say that "these teachers may try to impose a new history upon the children's actual history, in effect denying the legitimacy of these children's life experiences in Boston"(p. 453).

As Erickson and others have noted, the larger societal context and the power relations that exist between teacher and student play an important role in determining the ultimate effect that these discontinuities may have on students' academic achievement. Teachers who are committed to upholding the authority of mainstream culture often try to coerce children into using language in unfamiliar ways or malign the ways of talking that children bring to school. Eventually, their actions may lead to conflicts that affect the way teachers and students interact in classrooms. For example, Piestrup (1973) found that when teachers in first-grade classrooms corrected and negatively sanctioned African American children's nonstandard pronunciations, children increased their use of nonstandard English over the course of the school year. The opposite was true for African American children enrolled in classrooms where the teachers did not correct the children's language. Erickson (1987) argues that this kind of conflict fosters a teacher-student relationship devoid of trust:

> Teachers and students in such regressive relationships do not bond with each other. Mutual trust is sacrificed. Over time students become increasingly alienated from school. . . . The more alienated the student becomes, the less they persist in doing schoolwork. Thus, they fall further and further behind in academic achievement. The student becomes either actively resistant – seen as alienated and incorrigible or passively resistant – or fading into the woodwork as a well-behaved, low-achieving student. (p. 348)

Thus, when the patterns of language use or the patterns of social interactions that children bring to the school are ignored or devalued by their teachers, the students' academic development may suffer.

Language-use practices that originate in the school can also contribute to problems at home. In some cases, conflicts arise between parents and children over the values they feel are conveyed by language-use practices that their children bring from the school into the home. For example, many Eastside parents disapprove of teachers who, in their classroom discussions, emphasize the individual rights of students over the collective rights of the family. From their vantage point, the critical discussion of family matters by children and teachers at school represents a threat to the family structure and parents' authority. They resent what they construe to be teachers' interference in family business. Some even worry that teachers may encourage children to reveal information that may threaten their family's security (e.g., information about their immigration status, discipline practices). The ultimate impact of such a fear may lead to a general distrust of the school on the part of parents.

Wong-Fillmore (1991) provides a poignant example of the way language policies in some schools have threatened the socialization environment available to children at home. In a recent study that focused on the language-use practices in the homes of over 300 children of immigrant parents, she found that preschool-aged children who were enrolled in English-only or bilingual programs were particularly vulnerable to the loss of their primary language. As these children acquired English at school, they tended to rely more and more on English in their interactions with their parents at home. In the case of parents who did not speak or understand English, communication was impaired. Thus, a key means by which parents socialize and enculturate their children was seriously undermined. As Wong-Fillmore puts it,

> When parents are unable to talk to their children, they cannot easily convey to them their values, beliefs, understandings, or wisdom about how to cope with their experiences. They cannot teach them about the meaning of work, or about personal responsibility, or what it means to be a moral or ethical person in a world with too many choices and too few guide posts to follow. . . . When parents lose the means for socializing and influencing their children, rifts develop and families lose the intimacy that comes from shared beliefs and understandings.(p. 343)

To summarize, the picture of schooling as it is experienced by language-minority students is a distressing one. Driven by an overriding concern to assimilate students into the American mainstream, schools have not provided an optimal learning environment for language-minority students. English-language and basic-skills acquisition are viewed as the most important educational goals for this student population, with devastating results. Students with minimal or no knowledge of English are deprived of learning experiences in which they can use their native languages to express themselves fully. To aggravate matters, when children's teachers are not proficient in their students' native languages, they are not in a position to adequately judge the children's abilities because they fail to recognize the range of skills the children are manifesting as they converse in their native languages. Meaningful and relevant activities that entail the use of information and skills are rarely the focal point of instruction in classrooms of language-minority students. Recitation continues to be the discourse pattern that dominates in most U.S. classrooms, regardless of the ethnic and linguistic background of students. Finally, when classrooms are arenas for cultural conflict, differences in ways of talking become issues that threaten students' and teachers' ability to interact and learn from one another. Students may resist teachers' efforts to teach and teachers may dismiss these students as unteachable. Even students who comply with their teachers' wishes may be placed in positions that compromise their opportunity to learn outside of school. More specifically, when those students who acquiesce to the authority of the school and to messages of mainstream society abandon their native language and culturally appropriate forms of interacting, the socializing role of home and community may also be threatened.

CONNECTING HOME AND COMMUNITY TO THE SCHOOL

We believe that the circumstances that we have just described dissipate when schools begin to formally recognize and build upon the rich and varied language experiences and knowledge that are part of students' worlds at home and in their communities. This view, which we call a recognition perspective to learning and schooling, is based on the notion that the full range of minority children's experiences should be thought of as a resource for learning in schools, rather than as an impediment. We know that the basic principle we espouse is not new. In fact, a whole range of instructional approaches, including multicultural education, culturally responsive pedagogy, bilingual education, cross-cultural education, and multiethnic education, stress the importance of making schools places that draw upon the experiences of minority students. Unfortunately most of these approaches are also based on a limited view of children's experiences outside of school, one that tends to emphasize superficial aspects of their cultural background (e.g., holidays and food), which are then acknowledged at particular times of the year (e.g., Fifth of May celebrations and African American history month). Even when community and home-based enculturation practices are more fully incorporated into the curriculum, they are usually viewed as a means to instill in learners the mainstream discourse styles and literacy practices valued by white, middle-class educators. Thus, the home culture becomes little more than window-dressing that will be cast aside once students acquire these styles and practices.

In the discussion that follows, we draw upon others' analyses and definitions as well as on our own research and experiences to identify and elaborate on the attributes and challenges of the recognition perspective. We begin with three case-study descriptions of programs that have attempted to utilize language-minority children's linguistic and cultural experiences as instructional resources: a cross-age tutoring program, an after-school educational activity center, and a two-way bilingual education program. None of these programs operated flawlessly. Moreover, each was linked to a specific set of contexts and circumstances that make replication elsewhere problematic. Nevertheless what we learned from participating in and/or evaluating these programs has helped us to articulate the themes underlying the recognition perspectives that are discussed in the final chapter of this book.

CROSS-AGE TUTORING

In 1985, under the direction of Shirley Brice Heath, a small group of Stanford researchers and students, including Lucinda Pease-Alvarez, Olga Vásquez, and Marge Martus, instituted a cross-age tutoring project at Oakgrove Elementary School in the east side. Part of the rationale for this program arose from the realization that Eastside children play an important role in one another's socialization. Older children spend many hours of the day caring for their younger family members. In some single-parent households, children often assume the responsibilities of the absent parent. The Stanford group reasoned that by incorporating tutoring into the academic lives of the children, the program would capitalize on an authentic community-based context for learning language and literacy: The collaboration between tutors and tutees while reading and writing would closely resemble a familiar, home-based socialization/enculturation activity.

During the first year of the project the cross-age tutoring program involved 12 Mexicana/Latina fifth-grade girls and 22 Spanish-speaking first-grade boys and girls from the same ethnic background. Both older and younger children were excused from their regular classes to work together twice a week in a separate classroom. The girls were selected because they were not doing well in school and because they were infrequent and reluctant participants in regular classroom activities. The criteria used to select first-grade tutees varied; in most cases, first-grade teachers chose children whom they felt had seldom been read to outside of school.

During the two-week preparation period that preceded tutoring, the four Stanford participants read to the fifth-grade girls in small groups. The girls were encouraged to reflect on these book-reading events by watching themselves on video playbacks and identifying the analytic strategies that were used to talk about texts in their groups. After this initial training, the girls began tutoring younger students two times a week. Each tutoring session lasted 45 minutes and consisted mainly of reading aloud to the younger children, usually in Spanish. Before returning to their own classrooms, the tutors wrote in their field notebooks about their tutoring experience and discussed among themselves their successes and concerns.

In response to school-staff suggestions, the following year the program was expanded to include entire classrooms in cross-age tutoring. During the summer before the program's second year, Pease-Alvarez worked with fifth-sixth grade teacher Leslie Mangiola to help implement and develop cross-age tutoring and to study the interactions between tutors and tutees. The two women modified the original program on the basis of the previous year's experiences. For example, they decided to lengthen the preparation period for student tutors from two weeks to one month. The tutors' training would include viewing videotaped tutoring sessions, observing teachers working with kindergarten-age students, identifying the ways of talking about and using literacy that are characteristic of tutoring and teaching, reading a large number of children's books, and engaging in a variety of collaborative reading and writing activities including the use of computers (see Figure 12, a photograph of Pease-Alvarez helping students with a computer assignment). In addition, students would discuss their fieldnotes as a group, thereby increasing their opportunity for learning through interaction and self-reflection.

Once the school year began, Mangiola and Pease-Alvarez shared their observations and thoughts about tutoring (and other classroom activities) daily during recess and at lunch. They met biweekly with other teachers, and occasionally on their own, to view videotaped segments of tutoring sessions. These ongoing opportunities to reflect on actual classroom experiences led to improvements and innovations in the program. For example, over time, Mangiola and Pease-Alvarez changed their views about tutees' complaints, which they initially had interpreted as an indication that the project was failing. As the two collaborators worked through these complaints with tutors, they discovered that the pro-

Figure 12. Computers for the Stanford Reading and Writing Projects.

gram offered the children a natural forum for posing problems and reflecting upon their experiences during the discussion periods that followed tutoring. The following excerpt illustrates the kind of problem posing and problem solving that went on during these sessions.

> Ana: Pedro was a brat. He didn't want me to read to him. . . . All he did was hear himself talk in a tape recorder. Pedro said, "Why are you doing this?" And I said, "I'm teaching you guys to read and write."
>
> Linda: Maybe you could ask him why he doesn't want you to read to him? Is he bored?
>
> Ana: Yeah.
>
> Teacher: What would you do if you had a tutee . . .
>
> Linda: (interrupts teacher) Ask him what kind of things they like. Tell him what it's like when they grow up and they don't know what it's like to read or write.
>
> Teacher: Wha'd ya do with a kid that's bored?
>
> Iris: Ahm, get both your arms (makes hugging gesture).

Sara: Let him read to her 'cause sometimes some of the big kids they don't let their tutee read and that's what they want.

Teacher: You say he likes to color?

Mary: Let him color and tell you what the picture is about.

Sara: Or write down something.

Mario: Have him tell you a story about the pictures.

Iris: Or he could write words under it.

Discussions like this one provided students with frameworks for self-reflection. Often students who shared their experiences with others came up with their own solutions and insights. At one point, Ana, the tutor who was experiencing difficulties in the preceding exchange, was seriously considering abandoning her tutee, Pedro. After much deliberation, she reached her own solution: She decided to continue to work with Pedro because she was afraid that he would feel hurt if she were to abandon him. Tutoring Pedro was not easy. During the group discussions, Ana frequently brought up tutoring problems she had with him. But she persevered, developing tutoring strategies based on her own resources and on problem-solving sessions with her classmates and teachers.

The other tutors' self-reflections were evident in their fieldnote entries, end-of-the-year reports, and letters to the tutees' teachers. In the following entries, René sets forth the difficulties she was having with her tutee, Ken.

Ken was kinda wild today. He didn't want to come to the class or me reading to him. I hope he's not like this all year. If he is I'm changing. I don't really want to but if he's like that I'm gonna have too. Well I'll stay with him a little while. If he's good I'll stay with him. But I don't want it to be like this again.
[René, 11/11/87]

Today was kinda okay. He always hides from me when I go and pick him up and sometimes I don't like it when that happens. Maybe I should tell him that tommro – and I will – I hope he stops that when I tell him that and today i don't feel good and i think that why I didn't feel up with it. Well till tommro.

[René, 11/12/87]

Although René did not discuss these difficulties with other classmates, she struggled with her problems in ways that are similar to the strategies suggested in the discussion sessions that followed tutoring. She described her problems and her frustrations with Ken, and then she posited her own solution, "maybe I should tell him that tommro – and I will." Later in the year, her problems with Ken unabated, René sometimes verbalized her concerns to her classmates. She continued to experiment with her own solutions but also incorporated some of her peers' suggestions. Finally, she and Ken's teacher initiated a written dialogue. René submitted her fieldnote entries to the teacher weekly; the teacher, Peggy Smillen, responded by suggesting possible solutions. For example, in response to René's tentative decision to exchange Ken for another tutee, Peggy wrote the following note:

Dear René,

Did you decide to exchange tutees yet? I know Ken can be a handful. You've done a very good job so far, but if you feel you two aren't getting along well enough I trust your judgment. You are a good tutor and you deserve to work with someone who is willing to cooperate with you.

Love,
Peggy

Peggy also talked with her students (the tutees) about the problems the tutors described. Together, they brainstormed about ways to make tutoring a more pleasant experience for tutor and tutee alike. Some tutees, including Ken, decided to write "sorry notes" to their tutors. Judging from René's next two entries, Peggy's and the tutees' efforts made a difference.

Ken was good today. He listened to me when I was reading. He was real interested in alligators today. I hope he's interested in alligators tommoro and I hope he's twice as good as

155

he was today. Maybe I don't have to change now. But there's always tomorrow you know.

[René, 3/2/88]

Everything was perfect today. He wrote me a sorry letter and he even wrote about the book without even getting mad at me.

[René, 3/3/88]

Although tutoring Ken never became easy, René, like Ana, continued to rely on herself and others as she struggled through each tutoring session.

The tutors' definitions of literacy changed over the course of the school year. Sometimes teachers dealt with the topic of literacy overtly by discussing their own definitions and theories. In the context of cross-age tutoring, Mangiola talked to the tutors about how children develop as readers and writers. She showed overhead projections which detailed the development of children's writing, beginning with scribbling, working through pre-syllabic, alphabetic, and then conventional writing (Flores, 1982). She emphasized that their tutees' writing was properly regarded as writing despite the form it took, and she stressed that these young writers would eventually move on to other more recognizable types of writing.

On several occasions during tutoring, Mangiola and Pease-Alvarez had access to tutors' emerging views about literacy. Not surprisingly, these views were generally compatible with the perspective that informed the program as a whole. For example, most tutors agreed that kindergartners could read and write, although not always in conventional ways. One tutor, for example, distinguished between two different approaches to reading, by letter and from pictures, in her fieldnote entry:

Today I have Mónica she thought she dernt now how to read but I told her you can do it just reed it and she did she was riding it in spanish but it was in inglis. she try to reed by the leter and she got realy mixt up. and she stared to reed from the pichers.

[Marisol, 2/16/87]

Despite the differences in Mónica's approaches to reading, Marisol has chosen to call both approaches reading.

Interpreting their tutee's writing was a favorite activity during discussion sessions. Tutors would share what initially appeared to be undecipherable strings of letters written on large pieces of paper. Using some of the principles that Mangiola had discussed regarding the developmental nature of children's writing, tutors would "break" their tutees' written code. Afterwards, they would discuss any generalizable features of their tutees' writing (e.g., the use of "v" instead of "b", the reliance on consonants or, in the case of some Spanish speakers, on vowels).

Tutors also transmitted their views on literacy to their tutees. As the year progressed, they insisted that tutees do more reading and writing. Sometimes, as the fieldnote entry below indicates, they found themselves in the position of trying to convince tutees that they (the tutees) really could read and write.

> Today me and Leanore was arguing at one another and Leanore said that she could not read and I said that everybody could read. And I said, "Leanore, do you want to know how to read?" And she said, "Yes, I want to know how to read but I can't read." And I asked Marco [her classmate], "Do your tutee know how to read?" And he said yes. And I said, "See, Leanore, all kids know how to read."
>
> [Lisa, 8/26/87]

Sometimes the discussion sessions that followed tutoring focused on the appropriateness of what was being written or read. A particularly heated discussion followed the use of the book *In the Night Kitchen* by Maurice Sendak. Cecily had read the book several times to her tutee and came to the discussion asking what to do about the girl's delight in Sendak's illustrations of a naked child. Alice's and Javier's contrasting opinions reflect the opposing positions that characterize the broad issue of censorship in children's literature.

Cecily: I know it's a good idea to keep reading them their
favorite books over and over again. But I don't know

> if she wants me to read it again because she really
> likes the story or because she just likes to see the
> picture of the naked baby boy. She keeps wanting to
> go back to that and she just laughs and laughs.
> Alice: These parents don't send their kids to school to
> have us read them dirty books! They sure would be
> mad if they knew their kids were seeing books like
> that - and that we were reading them to them!
> Javier: Alice, it's just a baby. That's the way babies look.
> There's nothing wrong with that.

The discussion continued with Alice on the side of censorship and outrage and most of the rest of the class insisting that she was overreacting. Eventually, Alice concurred with the rest of the group that it was probably all right to read a book if you were reasonably sure that it would not offend your tutee. Discussions like this one show how the program challenged students to grapple with complex issues.

Interactions that were part of the cross-age tutoring program also directly affected all of the participating students' literacy development. In the context of collaborative activities that mattered to them, the tutors developed the kinds of literate behaviors that are often neglected in skills-based classrooms. In addition, because the tutors regularly documented, reflected, and acted upon their tutoring experiences, they gained valuable insights into the processes of teaching and learning. They began to understand that each act of teaching and learning must be considered and reconsidered if change is to take place. Tutors experienced firsthand the potential for power in learning at school – that it can be deliberate and well within their own control.

CONCERNS

Despite the program's overall success, it no longer exists. Leslie Mangiola left the classroom to work in an administrative position after the program's fourth year. Because she was no longer available to oversee the tutoring program, it was curtailed. The abrupt end to the program was in itself instructive because it highlighted the degree to which the circumstances that led to its establishment and refinement were part of its success. The collaborative working relationship between Mangiola and Pease-Alvarez, the time spent on working through problems, planning, and talking with students all contributed to the effectiveness of the project. All or some of these factors might be crucial for the success of future innovations. Determining which of the circumstances surrounding the cross-age tutoring program were most important in ensuring its success might yield the kind of knowledge that would help provide greater margins of success in future projects.

Cross-age tutoring capitalized on some home and community experiences. Other opportunities were missed, however. For example, prevailing patterns of socialization and/or child-raising in the community could have been a focus of the preparation phase. Having the tutors study patterns of talking and interacting between older and younger siblings and/or between parents and children would provide these students with information that might help them overcome recurring problems with their tutees. Teachers, too, would benefit from the class discussions that focused on these interactive patterns and on ways they might be successfully incorporated into school contexts. Future cross-age tutoring programs should include these types of collaborative, community-based research projects about language socialization as part of their agenda.

LA CLASE MAGICA: RECONFIGURING THE CURRICULUM

La Clase Mágica [The Magical Class] is another example of efforts aimed at making educational activity culturally and linguistically relevant to the participants. *La Clase Mágica* is a bilingual/bicultural reconfiguration of a computer-mediated literacy project developed by the Laboratory of Comparative Human Cognition (LCHC) at the University of California, San Diego. Situated on the grounds of a local church, *La*

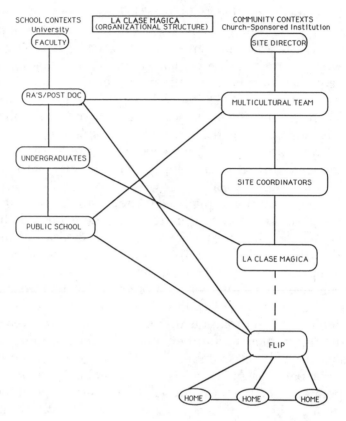

Figure 13. *La Clase Mágica* (organizational structure).

Clase Mágica, like its forerunner, Fifth Dimension, provides a context for examining and promoting learning and teaching through an activity system that combines play, new technology, and education. Elementary-school-age children from the surrounding Mexicano/Latino community voluntarily attend the program during after school hours to "play computers" while they practice a variety of literacy-mediated activities, such as writing letters via telecommunication. Undergraduate students taking university courses at UCSD participate as collaborators with the children in solving the problems posed by the games and at the same time are participants/observers in a "culture of collaborative learning"

(Cole and Nicolopoulou, 1991). This setting provided an opportunity for Olga Vásquez and her research staff to examine the literacy and language use practices of the children and their adult collaborators.

La Clase Mágica, established in 1989, grew out of a commitment among LCHC collaborators to serve linguistic-minority children. As a post-doctoral fellow under the mentorship of Michael Cole, Vásquez worked to solve a problem that had been plaguing the research efforts of LCHC for several years: The Fifth Dimension – an after-school, computer-based, educational activity – in northern San Diego County had been unable to recruit and retain Mexicano/Latino children (Cole, 1990).[2] LCHC collaborators suggested the establishment of a new Fifth Dimension site when Cole's students found an adjacent Mexicano/Latino community receptive and in need of educational services.

With the assistance of two community women and small cadres of UCSD undergraduate students taking classes with Vásquez, a Fifth Dimension site began to take shape at a nearby Catholic mission. The Fifth Dimension, developed for English-speaking elementary-school-age children, was destined for a drastic transformation from the moment that Vásquez approached the community. Many families drawn to the mission are primarily recent immigrants whose first language is Spanish. Many of the children come from young, low-income families who have been in the United States less than 15 years. When the idea of a new Fifth Dimension site was proposed in Spanish to community representatives, issues of culture and language featured prominently in the discussion. For example, the concept of a Fifth Dimension was itself problematic; in an early interaction with community members, one suggested *La Clase Mágica* as a more comprehensible name for the new program.

In addition to adopting the new name for the Fifth Dimension, the research team changed the program's underlying cultural assumptions and identity in response to the specific needs and desires of its target population. Spanish and Mexicano cultural knowledge became active ingredients in the new format. For six academic quarters, many of the activities were labeled "under construction" as staff, students, and researchers mapped out theoretical and conceptual foundations for culturally sensitive activities. Much of the structural and conceptual format of the Fifth Dimension remained intact, however. For example, the notion of a fantasy world represented by a 20-room maze with two to three games per room remained the same. The linkage between the community institution and the research/teaching program of the participating university also remained unchanged. *La Clase Mágica*, however, goes beyond its predecessor in that it is a bilingual, biliterate, and bicultural site serving a working-class, ethnic community less than a mile away, yet worlds apart from its neighboring Fifth Dimension site.

In redesigning the Fifth Dimension, the primary aim was to make the system and its activities contextually relevant to the children's lives. It is important to emphasize, however, that the team made the changes in a larger environment of restricted resources, a situation that mirrors the constraints found in most classrooms in the United States. Original tasks were constructed in English to serve an Anglo middle-class population, without references to the life experiences of minority children. Only three of the original computer games were in Spanish. The undergraduates, as well, reflected the racial and linguistic composition of the teaching work force. Relatively few spoke Spanish, and fewer still were of Mexican origin. The Mexican origin children, on the other hand, came from various linguistic and regional backgrounds. Additionally, some came from families who had lived in the area for generations, while others came from families who had recently migrated to the United States.

Transforming the Fifth Dimension involved considerably more than a simple act of translation from English to Spanish. Although informed throughout by traditional Mexican cultural knowledge, the Fifth Dimension's evolution into *La Clase Mágica* was not based solely on the children's home culture. Rather, it tapped the multiple knowledge sources available in the children's everyday lives. Whenever possible, content knowledge and skills from such diverse arenas as the family, church, sports, and dance groups were written into the guide sheets accompanying the games (Moll et al., 1992). Children were prompted to refer to common activities in Mexicano homes, such as story-telling, gardening, and verbal-play, when they wrote letters to *La Clase Mágica's* genial patron, *El Maga* [the Wizard].[3] The goal was to build upon the background knowledge of the children, while simultaneously introducing a new set of experiences in a second language. Thus, the skills and jargon of computer and telecommunication technology were interlaced with meanings and experiences cued by references to traditional Mexican folk tales, family histories, and notable figures in Mexican history. This strategy gave children a starting point for writing electronic messages and using the vocabulary of modern technology. In this way, children could draw on their personal experiences to write to *El Maga* and have a basis for interacting with the adults around them.

The team continually looked for alternative ways of connecting the children's existing knowledge base and language to new knowledge and new linguistic skills. Assured that "background knowledge helps make input comprehensible" and "language acquisition results from comprehensible input" (Krashen and Biber, 1989, p. 210) the team's concern was not with the acquisition of English but with developing ways to draw connections between the multiple skills and knowledge of the primary language and the many other uses of language and literacy available at *La Clase Mágica*. Given that most of the children spoke Spanish as their native language, their choice of language became an indicator of how the project was faring in its objective to provide free access to their background experiences.

Careful, critical analyses at several stages revealed a series of obstacles to the children's use of Spanish. In the first four quarters of the adaptation, the team found that the most definite and formidable obstacle to the children's free use of

Spanish lay in the structural relations among the participants. The use of English was being favored in almost all situations. If a bilingual adult engaged a child in Spanish, the
interaction was likely to shift to English if they turned their
attention to the computer (much of the software was in English), written materials (accompanying activity sheets were
in English), or to monolingual undergraduates. On those occasions when Spanish was used, it tended to be employed in
short discursive spaces. For example, if a child and adult began their interaction in Spanish, they automatically shifted
to English when they turned to the screen to read the directions of such English language games as "Where in the
World is Carmen San Diego."

Children's choice of language was also influenced by the
adults' ideological orientation. Although the community
women who joined the staff as site coordinators understood
English, they preferred the children to use Spanish. They
were concerned about the children's loss of Spanish and
feared impaired communication between the children and
their parents. The undergraduates, on the other hand, who
were collaborating with the children on solving the problems posed by the computer games, wanted to "take advantage of the opportunity to teach the children English so they
could compete in the outside world." Both groups' concerns
were valid; however, there was an apparent preference for
English at the beginning.

It was clear that in these earlier stages of the project, children thought they should speak English at *La Clase Mágica*.
English dominates most of their everyday experiences, and
it is certainly the language of choice at school. Although participation in *La Clase Mágica* is voluntary, some aspects of the
tasks are unavoidably formal and school-like. These elements were not lost on the children who, for the first several
quarters of the project addressed all of the adults as
"Teacher." Another plausible explanation for the children's
seeming preference for English is the low status accorded to
Spanish in the schools and the community at large (Commins, 1991). Many children quickly learn that using their na-

tive language is likely to earn them ridicule rather than prestige.

It is likely that in the earlier stages of the project, children were not using their full linguistic competency because they felt compelled to use English. As a consequence, adults sometimes misjudged the children's fluency in both languages. One child, who had been in the United States for a short period of time, was thought to be fluent in English because he was able to competently interact with undergraduates around the computer activities. However, when his interactions were carefully monitored through direct observation by a bilingual adult, it was clear that the child was not able to maintain a simple conversation in English. On closer examination, it was not clear how much of the interaction or, for that matter, how much of the game the child actually understood! The same was true of children whose fluency in English hid their competency in Spanish. Several second-generation children had a stronger command of Spanish than was apparently evident to the undergraduates.

In response to the persistence of English among *La Clase Mágica* participants, several changes were made. The first was to reinforce Spanish whenever resources were available. Bilingual undergraduates were asked to use Spanish exclusively at the site, unless the children themselves pursued the interaction in English. Bilingual or monolingual Spanish-language games were added to many of the rooms in the maze.[4] Two rooms were designated to specifically encourage language activities found in the homes and community. The story room, *Historiateca*, for example, was designed to encourage children to create stories in either language, to bring stories from home, or to read stories collected by the staff. The game room, *Actividades Tradicionales* [Traditional Activities], encouraged children to share with other participants games and diversions such as *lotería* [bingo-type boardgame] and *serpientes y escaleras* [chutes and ladders] practiced in their homes. Undergraduates with the greatest command of Spanish were asked to respond to the children's letters to *El Maga*. As these revisions became part of the daily routine of the project, the children's choice of language gradually shifted from the sole use of English to the use of English for specific purposes, such as in interactions with undergraduates while playing the computer games.

By the seventh academic quarter, children were making conscious decisions about which language to use with whom and in which domain. Although at this time, half of the undergraduates spoke some level of Spanish, the children continued to use English with them. At the same time, however, the team began to witness more freedom in the children's choice of Spanish when they were collaborating among themselves to solve game-related problems. By creating equal access to either language or cultural affiliation, the project was providing opportunities for children to exercise more choice, creating what Cummins (1989) would call greater student empowerment. The segment from an undergraduate's fieldnotes below indicates that at this stage of development, the children were juxtaposing learning with game problem-solving and the role of the undergraduates with teachers.

> Sara, possibly feeling excluded from our game, continued to interject while Nidia was playing. She spoke in Spanish to Nidia when Mary [a bilingual undergraduate student] was not directly helping her to solve the problem, or when she was just talking about the game, but when Mary became involved in the problem-solving, she used English and pointed to the items on the screen.
>
> [BP, 10/15/91]

Thus, children were using Spanish for play and English for learning activities.

To dispel any residual hierarchy in the role of the adults, their role was redefined and renamed as simply Amigos/ Amigas [friends]. Improvements also were made with the assistants who helped *El Maga* write letters to the children, so that when the eighth quarter began, adults were defined as friends and *El Maga* was a masterful, bilingual wizard whose manipulation of regional varieties of Spanish instantly touched a responsive chord in at least one child, who exclaimed, *"Ah, ahora tenemos una Chola para maga,"* ["Oh! Now we have a Chola (female member of a Chicano youth culture) for Wizard!"].

These changes further affected the use of Spanish and English at *La Clase Mágica*. The team began noting that the children's use of Spanish was in transition from the social sphere into the literacy activities. Children's previous reluctance to use Spanish had prevented the adults from observing their literacy skills in the first language; however, once the children began writing to *El Maga* in Spanish on their own, adults' assessment of children's skills greatly improved. An interesting phenomenon noted at this time was that children were relying more on the written language on the computer monitor and on the guide sheets that accompany the games. They were taking more time to read the directions on the monitor instead of incessantly pressing on the keys to move forward. On one occasion, a nine-year-old boy spent three site visits reading a complicated game manual, so that he could figure out how to play a game that interested him. The adult English speakers could provide no help in deciphering the manual's excessively technical language.

Although the project has a long way before it structurally supports the use of both languages equally in advanced critical thinking skills, the children's responses at *La Clase Mágica* indicate that they perceive themselves as having a choice concerning which language to use. In the ninth quarter of the project, children were visibly comfortable using either language. Their perception of the equal value of both languages expressed by Rina, a seven-year-old child who, when asked why she wanted to speak two languages, responded,

. . . y a mí me gusta hablar inglés. Yo debo hablar inglés porque a veces no me acuerdo como decir bombero como dicerlo en español.

. . . I like to speak English. I should speak English because sometimes I can't remember how to say [the word for] fireman in Spanish.

Rina understood that by speaking two languages, she had a broader system from which to make meaning. If she did not know the word in one language, she could rely on her other language to help make herself understood.

When children experience complete freedom in the choice of language, an optimal learning condition is created that directly enhances their ability to learn and perform academically. Given the opportunity to freely tap their cultural and linguistic resources, children will, as Rina described, choose communicative value over form. They will push the limits of their ability to express themselves rather than staying bound to an incomplete message shaped by the lack of fluency in a language. Their critical thinking skills are enhanced not by speaking a variety of languages but by the ability to use resources at their disposal to negotiate meanings in problem-solving activities (Hymes, 1972). The work at *La Clase Mágica* shows that capitalizing on the cultural and linguistic re sources that children bring to the learning environment makes more sense than beginning with a clean slate. Using the multiple skills and knowledge of the primary language in the learning setting not only facilitates the acquisition of the second language and its literacy, it also helps to develop doers and thinkers rather than passive receptors of knowledge.

CONCERNS

The success of *La Clase Mágica* does not, however, necessarily mean that it, or some version of it, should be instituted indiscriminately. Creating a culturally responsive approach to learning entails its own set of tensions and structural obstacles. For example, the knowledge bases in paired communities may not be compatible.[5] Adapting the curriculum to fit that of the corresponding community is a slow and open-ended process. Analysis and reanalysis of the progress is the best indicator of whether children are being given the opportunity to use their own background skills in acquiring new ones. Reassessing *La Clase Mágica's* bilingual/bicultural components in the program's early stages indicated that it was not a true bilingual/bicultural site. This was partially due to the role of Spanish in the program's activities. The team had initially been reluctant to insert Spanish words and sentences in the adapted guide sheets because the benefits and drawbacks of code-switching in oral and written language have not been conclusively identified by social science researchers. Moreover, given limitations in available linguistic resources, the children participating in *La Clase Mágica* could not truly choose a language in which to interact with the students, *El Maga*, or even the literacy-mediated tasks. It is also important to remember that providing a culturally responsive curriculum necessarily involves many levels of input from the community, the university, the home, and the research team. On-going linkages among these groups are fundamental to an accurate portrayal and incorporation of the children's background experiences.

BILINGUAL EDUCATION IN NORTHERN CALIFORNIA

This section focuses on a program that recognizes Spanish as a resource that should be made available to all students, regardless of their ethnicity or native-language proficiency. This approach is a radical departure from the conventional treatment of minority languages in most bilingual education programs across the country (McGroarty, 1992; Pease-Alvarez and Hakuta, 1992), where the goal is to transition children into mainstream classes where English is the exclusive medium of instruction. In these programs, the students' primary language is used mainly to facilitate content-area instruction; in some cases, it is also the medium for initial literacy instruction. Once students in bilingual programs acquire the level of English proficiency deemed sufficient for pursuing the rest of their studies in English, they no longer receive instruction in their native language. For many minority children, participating in bilingual programs may ultimately accelerate the loss of proficiency in their native language (Crawford, 1989).

In increasing numbers, educators are asserting that this form of bilingual education is a terrible waste of linguistic resources. Instead of coming out of school fully proficient in two languages, some language-minority children run the risk of leaving school less proficient in what was once their native language. Even those who retain their proficiency in their native languages have little or no opportunity to further develop these languages once they enter middle schools, where English prevails as the language of instruction. Tragically, the social and cognitive benefits associated with bilingualism may no longer be available to those language-minority students who are in the process of losing one of their languages. Although schools play little or no role in ensuring the development of bilingualism in these students, they do at least pay lip service to promoting bilingualism in monolingual English-speaking children. Ironically, once these children reach high school, they are encouraged to add to their language repertoire by taking foreign language classes, while language-minority students enrolled in most bilingual education programs are encouraged to replace their native languages with English. Crawford sums up the basic inequity of this policy as "additive bilingualism for English speakers and subtractive bilingualism for language minorities" (1989, p. 164).

Additive bilingualism is the goal of the two-way or Spanish immersion bilingual education program available to Anglo and Mexican-descent students living in the town of Lawson, California. Native English speakers and native Spanish speakers of Mexican descent who are enrolled in this program spend all but 20 minutes of every school day in classrooms where Spanish is the exclusive medium of instruction. Teachers address all students in Spanish and all students are first formally taught to read and write in Spanish. Teachers in this program use only Spanish, even when addressing monolingual English-speaking students who are not students in their classes. Some even extend their use of Spanish into the domain of the teachers' room and school office. Initially, English monolingual students participating in the program address their teachers in English. By second grade, however, all students are expected to use only Spanish in the classroom.

Under the sponsorship of the Organization for Economic Cooperation and Development and the U.S. Department of Education, Pease-Alvarez conducted a qualitative case study of this program. Because two-way programs represent a departure from the prevailing deficit views of bilingualism that underlie bilingual education, one of the goals of this case study was to trace the emergence of such a program. Pease-Alvarez's interest in this subject was further motivated by her realization that Lawson, like many rural communities with an economic structure that is dominated by a few Anglo growers, was not known for having a population with positive views about bilingualism and/or ethnic minorities prior to the establishment of the two-way program. The following is a brief account of how the Lawson program evolved.

Bilingual education had been part of the educational scene in Lawson, a small (population approximately 8,500), politically conservative city in northern California, for 12 years prior to the development of the two-way program. The overarching goal of the initial program, which was established in 1979, was to transition limited English proficient (LEP) students into the regular curriculum. According to former program participants, teachers barely proficient in Spanish themselves seldom used this language in their classrooms. In early 1980s, Arturo Vargas, a new teacher working with migrant children, began laying the groundwork for a bilingual program based on a very different view of language and culture. Vargas envisioned a program that would provide Anglo and Latino children with opportunities to develop oral fluency and literacy in Spanish and English. According to Vargas, primary language instruction for Latino students is a key factor in insuring their academic success, eventual mastery of English, and high self-esteem. Vargas' own experience had led him to this conclusion:

I found that kids from Mexico who came to school with a solid education in Spanish . . . were successful in school and later with English. . . . I wanted to duplicate this experience for LEP kids. . . . Also, living in Texas and Arizona speaking my primary language wasn't a healthy thing to do. I ended up in the principal's office getting hit for using Spanish.

Well aware that he needed district, parental, and overall community support to ensure the program's success, Vargas began by enlisting the aid of the district superintendent, John Sweeney. Once convinced of the benefits of bilingual education for Latino and Anglo students, Sweeney authorized Vargas and the district's two elementary school principals to write the Title VII grant that funded the bilingual education program from 1983–8. According to Vargas, Sweeney continued to give him free rein to seek out ways to improve and build on the program once it was funded. Sweeney, now retired, described his management style as providing others with the autonomy and freedom to implement their own ideas, on the grounds that "accountability and responsibility go hand in hand with autonomy." Vargas also worked hard to educate the school board about the benefits of his approach to bilingual education:

My strategy (he explained) was to be a public relations person and to educate the board a little at a time. Board meetings weren't a means of educating them as much as taking them to lunch, to (a Spanish language institute in) Cuernavaca, giving them articles, taking them to CABE (California Association for Bilingual Education) conferences, and to visit other schools with good programs.

Vargas characterized his initial efforts to educate board members as a struggle, but he reported that once educated, they became strong advocates of bilingual education programs that were committed to the maintenance and development of Spanish for Anglo as well as Latino students.

In his efforts to secure the support of the Lawson community and parents, Vargas became a key figure in community activities. He joined the Rotary Club and organized a sister-cities program with Cuernavaca. He gave presentations on bilingual education to Kiwanis, church groups, and a variety of other organizations. In addition, he developed a positive and enduring relationship with the staff of the local newspaper. The paper continues to spotlight the accomplishments of the bilingual program to this day. He enlisted parent support through his many community activities, and he also organized meetings to inform parents first about bilingual education and later about Spanish immersion education.

Vargas' efforts to promote bilingualism in the Lawson community did not stop once the grant was secured. He invited board members to staff development programs funded under the grant and he made sure that board members traveled to Cuernavaca to participate in a Spanish-language training program that was available to participating teachers. He carefully screened applicants and selected teachers who were committed to the goals of dual language development for all students. He met with teachers regularly to talk about the program's goals and its future direction. Many of these teachers currently hold administrative positions in Lawson, either at the district level or at school sites. They continue to uphold the goals of the bilingual program.

Disappointed with the level of Spanish that Anglos learned in the bilingual program and the tendency for all children to use more English than Spanish in the classroom and on the playground, Vargas began to investigate alternative approaches that would lead to the development of bilingualism in both Anglo and Latino students. Initially, he and the bilingual teachers in Lawson discussed articles describing second language immersion programs in Canada and the United States. Later, these articles were circulated among district administrators, school board members, and parents. Vargas started informing the community, the school board, and school administration about Spanish immersion programs. With the administrators' backing, Vargas invited an expert on Spanish immersion education to make a series of three presentations to parent audiences in the spring of 1986. Afterward, he took a group of ten Anglo parents to a nearby community to visit a Spanish immersion program. It was a highly effective strategy. As one parent explained, "We were excited about immersion education before our visit. But we were convinced afterward." In May of 1986, Vargas and 20 parents, most of them Anglo, approached the school board to request a pilot Spanish immersion classroom at the kindergarten level for the 1986–87 school year. Prior to the meeting, parents persuaded one of the bilingual kindergarten teachers to agree to teach a Spanish immersion class if the board approved the plan. The board did so, with the stipulation that immersion classes would receive no additional financial support beyond what was offered to regular bilingual classes. Parents raised funds to buy computers, Spanish-language materials, and books and to defray the costs of sending the immersion teacher to conferences on immersion education. They also recruited new parents into the program and worked with district administrators to determine criteria for admitting children into the Spanish Immersion Program. By this time, the parents interested in immersion education had formed a Lawson chapter of Advocates for Language Learning (L.A.L.L.), a national organization composed mainly of Anglo parents interested in promoting the spread of immersion education throughout the country. John Dean, the president of L.A.L.L., says that his vision "is to have immersion education in 50 percent of the schools in this country because kids in immersion programs achieve academically as well as or better than if they were educated in English, plus they learn Spanish. They get everything and then some."

One grade level has been added to the Spanish Immersion Program each year since 1988. At the time of Pease-Alvarez's study, the program included classes in grades kindergarten through third. Teachers used only Spanish with their students both in and out of the classroom. Another teacher, aide, or parent joined the classroom to offer 20 to 40 minutes of English-language development, which usually consisted of reading to the children in English or overseeing a hands-on activity. Students also used English when they participated in the range of special activities available to the entire school (e.g., music classes, art classes, assemblies). Initial literacy was introduced in Spanish; teachers had decided to wait until the second half of third grade before providing literacy instruction in English.

A number of factors contributed to the establishment of the Spanish Immersion Program. Arturo Vargas' vision and efforts were critically important. He made sure that key figures in the decision-making process shared his conviction that Latino and Anglo children should have access to programs where they develop Spanish and English. He communicated his plan to teachers, administrators, parents, and community members and convinced them of its merit. Although his success is partly attributable to personal characteristics, he employed strategies that could be adopted by others. For example, to convince those in power of the efficacy of an educational approach that capitalizes on language-minority students' linguistic resources, he backed up his ideas with articles and information about current programs. He also brought in experts to work with administrators and teachers. Moreover, he worked gradually, carefully laying the groundwork for each innovation that he planned. He began by presenting his ideas to key figures (e.g., the superintendent and school board members) and then showed them effective programs and provided them with opportunities to talk to experts in the field.

Parents, especially Anglo parents, and teachers who had been at the center of change, particularly those who were active in implementing the Spanish Immersion Program, felt that their opinions and views had been incorporated into the school decision-making process. One parent who had spearheaded the parent effort to establish a Spanish Immersion Program was proud to have had such an impact on the district. In fact, he is committed to exerting parental influence in ways that traditionally have been denied to parents (e.g, in setting hiring policies). Like other Lawson parents and Spanish immersion teachers, he has become part of a national effort to promote second-language learning through immersion education.

This atmosphere of joint decision-making and shared responsibilities was fostered by superintendent Sweeny's commitment to giving his staff free rein. Moreover, Sweeny added his personal support to Vargas and the teachers he hired as they worked to implement and improve upon the bilingual program. The current superintendent continues to back the efforts of those involved in extending the scope of the program to include English-only classrooms.

Another strategy which helped insure the establishment of the program was the consistent emphasis on inclusion rather than exclusion. Arturo Vargas involved board members and administrators in his efforts to obtain the Title VII grant that supported the bilingual program from 1983 to 1988. In turn, program and school administrators, as well as bilingual and Spanish immersion teachers, have encouraged the involvement of nonbilingual teachers in the activities of both the Spanish immersion and bilingual program. Nonbilingual teachers, many of whom do not support program objectives, are invited to their inservice trainings. In addition, materials and curricula that have been developed by and for bilingual staff are available to regular classroom teachers. Currently, plans are being made for bilingual teachers to team with nonbilingual teachers to offer Spanish language instruction. The rationale for these inclusive measures is twofold: First, nonbilingual staff members who team teach with bilingual teachers may become more aware of the benefits of Spanish language instruction; and second, bilingual and immersion staff (as well as the superintendent) want to expand these programs to include more Anglo students.

That Vargas and a core group of teachers shared a similar vision for the program is significant. Despite Vargas' critical role as a catalyst, many key players did not need him to convince them of the benefits of an instructional approach that highlights the use and learning of Spanish. As Gerry Adams, a kindergarten teacher, put it, "Many of us have been committed to bilingual education and dual language maintenance for years." Interviews with activists dedicated to providing Lawson children with a high-quality bilingual program revealed that many of these individuals' previous experiences led to or enhanced their appreciation of cultural and linguistic diversity. Program proponents include former Peace Corps volunteers, the sons and daughters of farm workers living in California and the Southwest, immigrants from countries where bilingualism is respected, and people who have lived abroad for extended periods of time – especially in Latin American countries.

The community context was also an important factor. School-related issues do not appear to have led to divisiveness across ethnic boundaries in Lawson; in other communities, intergroup hostilities typically have accompanied efforts to introduce bilingual education and desegregation (Pease-Alvarez, 1989). No doubt Lawson's receptivity is due in part to the relatively small number of Latinos involved, mostly Mexican immigrants who live in and around the area. Interviewees also seemed to feel that the white growers and business people in the area despite their political conservatism, were not as exploitative as their counterparts in the Southwest. As one Chicano teacher noted, "Even the most rednecked ones [here] are not as rednecked as they are in other places." Perhaps the conflicts that typically characterize interethnic relationships between groups of people with unequal status and power were less prevalent in this area because of the relatively benevolent attitudes of those in power.

Finally, the size of the school district may have influenced the development of bilingual education in Lawson. Obviously, a small program operating in a small district (Lawson has only two elementary schools) can make certain kinds of changes more easily than can a very large district. The greater likelihood of direct communication between administrators and teachers in a small district contributes to the success of inclusionary strategies such as the articulation of shared goals and joint decision making. Because the Lawson Latino population has not yet reached the proportions found in larger school districts, administrators have not had to significantly enlarge their bilingual staff, nor have classroom ethnic ratios changed dramatically. Lawson class ratios show more integration with between 60 percent and 30 percent Anglo students.

CONCERNS

By all standard measures, the development of the bilingual and Spanish immersion programs in Lawson ranks as an outstanding success. Not only have academic goals been met, as measured by gains in students' achievement scores over the years, but the community as a whole has come to recognize and value the linguistic resources of its minority population. Certain features that led to the institutionalization of this program could be considered worrisome, however. For example, Anglo parents, not Latino parents, played a critical role in generating the needed support and resources that led to the establishment of the Spanish Immersion Program, and they continue to wield more influence over the decision-making process. Some Anglo parents are now demanding a say in the hiring and firing of Spanish immersion teachers. This activist stance has spilled over into the classroom, as well. Some teachers resent the intrusion of overzealous Anglo parents who question or complain about particular classroom activities. This kind of intervention seldom characterizes Mexicano parents' interactions with the schools. This unequal involvement and access to schooling across the two parent groups could have far-reaching implications in an integrated instructional setting. At the very least, there is irony in an instructional program that recognizes the linguistic resources of a minority group in a school context where the voices of majority group members appear to prevail.

SUMMARY

Although these three case studies are unusual, they are instructive in helping us to conceptualize an educational setting in which educators recognize and build upon the background experiences of their students. Although teachers seldom have the institutional support that is evident in the three cases described here, much can be learned from these programs about how to use language and culture as resources in the classroom. We feel teachers hold the key to social change that is inevitable in view of the changing demographics in our society. And although we acknowledge that societal forces can exert a negative influence on students' ability to do well in school and that teachers cannot be totally responsible for their students' academic performance, teachers do spend six long and precious hours of the day with students.

At no other time in history have teachers had such a critical mandate. As these case studies have demonstrated, teachers cannot single-handedly reshape the American educational system, they need the assistance of parents, school boards, and other community institutions. Serving the needs of a diverse student population is a complex, deliberate, and dynamic process. A packaged approach applied intact to every situation and regional location will not work. Effective change requires involvement by relevant local institutions at a variety of levels (e.g., the home, the school, and the university). Revitalizing education to make it relevant to all groups is a project in which all participants – parents, teachers, paraprofessionals, policymakers, children, and researchers – must cooperate, jointly shaping goals and objectives to guide the process of change.

Another lesson we learn from these cases is that providing a culturally responsive education is not a piecemeal undertaking. It requires a fundamental reordering of the organization of instruction. Both instructors and the content of their instruction must be imbued with a sense of respect and appreciation for differences in background experiences and world views. Bridging these differences is one of the greatest challenges teachers face today. A view of language and culture as a resource is a first step in the direction of change. As the voices of the children from the cross-age tutoring program and *La Clase Mágica* testify, language-minority children are not refugees from impoverished "language environments." Their linguistic repertoires and cultural affiliations draw on their home, school, and community experiences. And, in contrast to conventional wisdom, children in a bilingual/bicultural environment are able to learn and flourish using two languages.

Chapter 7

Meeting the challenges of diversity

Our descriptions of the language practices of Eastsiders contribute to a positive portrayal of the socialization experiences available to a community of learners. The children and adults who engage in the interactions we describe are resourceful participants in a complex and dynamic social milieu. They make optimal use of their social, cultural, and linguistic resources to meet their own needs as well as those of their families and friends. Moreover, as they strive to make sense of an unfamiliar culture and language, they further their own intellectual development in ways that are largely unavailable to monolingual English speakers living in predominantly middle- or upper-class communities.

The following description of Rosalina, an Eastsider, serves as a final metaphor for our work. Although this case depicts an unusual individual, it serves as an example of the kind of student educators might dismiss if they are not mindful of the "hidden" potential behind an apparent incongruity of socioeconomic and family background. Although Rosalina is succeeding as a college student in an institution where few Latinos have succeeded previously, many of the attributes that make her special also characterize other Eastside children.

ROSALINA: CHININA
AT BERKELEY

Like many other first generation children, Rosalina Calderón spoke only Spanish when she entered school in the United States. She spent kindergarten through second grade in Mexican schools and in 1978 along with her three older brothers and a sister immigrated to Lincoln City. Her parents had already immigrated to the area two years prior to her arrival. During those two years, Rosalina and an older sister lived with relatives in Uruapán, Michoacán, waiting for their parents to earn enough money to pay for their children's trip north. The three brothers who were left in the hometown of Las Casitas with their grandparents had not been as fortunate as their sisters. They had had to interrupt their studies to help out with the chores around the farm. Unfortunately, they never made up for lost time once they entered school in the United States. All three eventually dropped out of high school.

By saving diligently from the meager pay she earned as a maid and borrowing from her sister who taught her to clean American homes, Rosalina's mother was able to add to the small amount of money she pinched from her husband's salary in order to reunite her family. She and the baby had joined her husband, who after many years of following the migrant stream up the California-Washington trail, had decided to settle down in the east side. Every year since the children could remember, their father had left the family for extended periods – *para irse al norte* [to go to the United States] – and it was the first time since he had entered the United States some 20 years earlier that the entire family was about to live together. However, the family was not to achieve a stable homelife in their adopted country for the next five years. They were deported en masse four times when Mr. Calderón was caught driving while drinking, and it was discovered that the family was illegally residing in the United States. When Rosalina was in junior high school, her father was arrested during a visit to Mexico. After serving five years in a Mexican prison, he returned to the east side in time to see Rosalina graduate from high school.

Chinina, as her family called her, entered school concerned that she did not understand what was being said around her but nevertheless enthusiastic about all the possibilities that her new experiences would bring. *"Me sentía mal"* ["I felt bad"], she said, when students laughed at her English pronunciation and felt even worse when she could not understand the lessons in English. Recalling the pain of those early years, she said,*"Entre más te frustras más quieres aprender"* ["the more you get frustrated the more you want to learn"]. She wasn't daunted. She wanted to learn so she pestered her Migrant Education teachers at recess and lunch for extra help.

Although her older brothers and sister occasionally translated for her parents or other adults, Chinina was the most comfortable and capable in the role of family translator. After only a few years in the United States, she was translating for her mother's extensive network of friends and family. *"Me prestaba mi mamá"* ["my mother loaned me out"], she said, about helping others to negotiate the English language and Anglo institutional culture.

Chinina's mother, Doña Beatriz, *conocía a todos* [knew everyone], helping them with their religious, medicinal, and social needs. She was known in the community for leading the *novena* in celebration of a death in the family. Because Chinina *se le pagaba a su mamá* [tagged along with her mother] she got to know many people in the community. Through them, often in the role of their spokesperson, she met representatives from a variety of institutions, acquiring their jargon and the norms of interactions as a function of her mediation. In 1987, when a Stanford graduate student surveyed the social networks of Mexicano classmates at her high school, Rosalina had the most extensive and dense networks in the study. In other words, she had many individuals to whom she could turn to for her socioemotional and academic needs.

Chinina's educational journey was not an easy one. She and her youngest brother were the first and only ones of the six children to graduate from high school; the others dropped out to help with the family's expenses, get married, or avoid the stressful demands of coursework for which they were not prepared. She earned high marks in high school but barely made the college entrance requirements. She was short in Advanced Placement courses and scored average on the SAT (Scholastic Aptitude Test). However, she had an outstanding record in extracurricular activities, was a fluent Spanish/English bilingual, and received glowing recommendations from her academic mentors. She danced for a local Mexican folkloric ballet, participated in Toastmasters debates, and was actively involved in church and community activities. All through school she studied hard and took on odd jobs to pay for her expenses and to help out her mother.

While still in high school Rosalina worked for Vásquez transcribing data. She also helped her to broker the cultural and linguistic patterns of the community. Frequently, she pointed out the cultural meanings of interactions, specifying the intent of indirect statements. As a sophomore in high school, her future goal was to become a doctor in her community. Now in her senior year at the University of California at Berkeley, she is indebted to her family for the sacrifices they have endured so that she could attend college. Everyone in her family, including her younger siblings, contributed to her success by filling the economic and socioemotional void that her absence created.

Although Rosalina has confronted and continues to confront many barriers to academic success, she has drawn upon a range of resources both in and out of her immediate community to negotiate a difficult journey through a school system that has been inaccessible to many of her friends and family members. Clearly her success can be attributed to her personal efforts. However, her position in her family structure, age of entry into the educational system, and her extended network of support, made it possible for her to seek out and take advantage of available opportunities. She received the benefit of not having to support the family as had been the charge of the older siblings so that she could concentrate on her studies. To make sure she continued her education, the family pooled their resources to help her. For example, family gatherings, which formerly were held in the east side, now take place in a park located a few miles from Chinina's dormitory. The family decided on this change in their routine so that Chinina would be sure to spend time with her various family members. For her last birthday, everyone, including aunts, uncles, and siblings, pitched in to buy Rosalina clothing for the upcoming academic year. Her parents and other family members regularly bring groceries and other items that they purchase at discount outlets to Chinina and her roommates.

We contend that Rosalina's success is largely a function of the support she receives from her extended network of family and friends, as well as her own determination to succeed. Her ability to successfully juggle her multiple cultures and languages, rather than abandoning one for another, has allowed her to benefit from and contribute to the family support structure. In addition, her experiences as a cultural broker for members of her social network has helped her face the cultural and linguistic sophistication of academia. It is likely that the vocabulary as well as the ease in dealing with novel situations she acquired as family interpreter has made it easier for her to accomplish her course assignments and oral presentations. She continues to be a social activist on campus as a member of Chicano/a student social and academic organizations. Unfortunately, limited economic resources including the multitude of factors that contribute to the scarcity of these resources have made it difficult for other members of Rosalina's family to pursue academic advancement.

As the previous chapter has shown, attempts to move toward an approach to schooling that builds upon the social, cultural, and personal worlds of language minority students like Rosalina is a complicated endeavor. Many would argue that the goal we advocate for schooling is impossible given that public school education in the United States values the knowledge and skills that are generally available to the middle and upper classes. Our own experience and that of others have provided glimpses of classrooms and programs where ethnic minority students' lives outside of school are viewed as instructional resources. Based on these experiences, we are somewhat optimistic that educators can use knowledge about their students' communities as an effective instructional resource. In the discussion that follows, we articulate a set of themes that should be part of the knowledge base that teachers and administrators draw upon when they attempt to utilize students' sociocultural backgrounds as instructional resources.

CONSIDERING A VARIETY OF CULTURES AND CONTEXTS

While teachers certainly realize that school is a new experience for most first-time students and that it takes time to learn the norms of behavior expected in this setting, they may not know that school is just one of many culture or reference groups available to children from linguistically and culturally diverse backgrounds. Like children everywhere, children who speak a language other than English in their homes are shaped by their families, peer groups, secondary institutions, immediate neighborhoods, and their families' informal and formal social networks. What makes these experiences different in the context of language-minority groups is that they are embedded in two or more languages or cultures. For example, the Mexicano children of Eastside move in and out of multiple worlds, each with its own set of cultural and linguistic norms and expectations. Besides school, these worlds include after-school sports, church, commercial establishments, parents' workplaces, neighborhoods, the predominantly Anglo neighborhoods that surround the east side, and the homes and communities of relatives and friends who live as far away as Mexico, Oregon, and Washington. From an early age children learn to apply knowledge and skills acquired in these contexts to work through the problems they encounter in everyday life. Frequently, they play a critical role in gaining access to institutional culture as they collaborate with others in figuring out the meanings of verbal or written texts that originate in schools, governmental agencies, banks, and other secondary institutions. As interpreters children often help adults to negotiate these different contexts.

Unfortunately, educators seldom seem to consider the complexity of their students' experiences in a multilayered network of cultures and reference groups. Simply grounding a program in one aspect of students' experiences is no guarantee that it will function smoothly. In some cases, students' resistance or refusal to participate in multicultural programs that highlight specific features of their native cultures or languages are sometimes grounded in their perceptions of these programs as irrelevant to their experience as participants in other cultural milieus. In case studies of Australian educational programs and classes that language-minority students attend, Kalantzis, Cope, Noble, and Poynting (1990) found that course offerings that incorporated aspects of these students' languages or cultures were stigmatized. Language-minority students felt these courses were largely irrelevant for their future academic careers. Because these courses were not required for university entrance or even for the successful completion of secondary school, language-minority students and their parents, most of whom were interested in enhancing their academic opportunities, saw no reason to take them. Eventually, several of these course offerings were removed from their schools' curricula.

A recognition perspective to schooling at least theoretically opens the possibility for students and teachers to view students' background experiences as an integral and *valued* component of the learning milieu in schools. In this way, teachers and students do not have to feel compelled to choose one cultural affiliation, reference group, and/or set of experiences over another. For this ideal scenario to occur, educators must understand and integrate in fundamental ways the multiple contexts in which students operate. They must consider ways of enhancing students' ability to both value and negotiate the complicated cultural milieu of the school, home, and society. Favoring the values, languages, and ways of acting of one group over others in curricular and instructional practices must be avoided at all costs. When it comes to determining the role of languages and discourse practices in this endeavor, the job of educators is to help all students to appreciate and benefit from the mastery of multiple languages and discourses, not just that of the school or that of the home culture.

LEARNING ABOUT THE COMMUNITY: MAKING THE CURRICULUM RELEVANT

In their attempts to honor the cultural affiliations of students, multicultural approaches to education have tended to focus more on the generic features of a given culture (e.g., celebrations, foods, and costumes) and less on the unique experiences of members of a particular group or community living in this country. In fact what it means to be a member of a cultural group in the United States context is seldom addressed in the curriculum; even more rarely is consideration given to the specific attributes and circumstances of a cultural group in a particular community. For example, groups with a 20-year history in the United States develop patterns of interaction and norms that are different from those who have settled elsewhere or who have remained in their native country. Even Mexican origin students who live in the same community and share the same socioeconomic standing have access to very different learning experiences because of variability in their regional and generational backgrounds. Moreover, the local communities where they settle change over time in response to economic trends, immigration patterns, and political actions. Consequently, teachers and administrators need in-depth knowledge of their students and their students' communities. They cannot afford to rely exclusively on secondary sources and hearsay regarding the experiences and characteristics of a particular group. Moreover, they must constantly update this knowledge if they are to stay current with changes in their students and their students' communities.

One way in which this can be accomplished is by teachers and university-based researchers collaborating on ethnographic studies of students' communities. This in turn can lead to meaningful connections between curriculum and community. For example, Luis Moll (1992) and his colleagues at the University of Arizona have spent several years collaborating with teachers so that they can better understand and utilize students' cultural resources in classroom settings. Underlying this work is the principle that "the students' community represents a resource of enormous importance for educational change and improvement" (p. 21). Together, teachers and researchers have interviewed parents and other community members to identify the information and skills that are available to Mexicano households through an elaborate set of social networks that connects these households to other households and institutions. This set of information and skills, which Moll and his colleagues term "funds of knowledge," consists of the "cultural practices and bodies of knowledge and information that households use to survive, to get ahead or to thrive" (p. 21). Examples of funds of knowledge available to families that were uncovered by the research team include information about the cultivation of plants, seeding, water distribution and management, animal husbandry, veterinary medicine, ranch economy, mechanics, carpentry, masonry, electrical wiring, fencing, folk remedies, herbal cures, midwifery, archaeology, biology, and mathematics.

Teacher-researchers participating in this work have organized their curriculum around these funds of knowledge. They have sought out and used the expertise of community members to teach them and their students about the specific areas of specialization that they have then built into their lessons. For example, Moll (1992) describes a teacher who developed a social network within her students' community of experts who contributed to a curriculum unit on construction. Experts included the students, who had participated in various research projects about construction, their parents and relatives, the parents of other students in the school, and resources that were available to the teacher through her own set of social networks (e.g., other school staff members, community members, university personnel). These experts shared their experiences in construction, participated in student-led interviews, and helped students design and implement their own construction projects. In essence, this teacher worked to develop an approach to schooling that Moll describes as "teaching through the community" (p. 23).

Similar research collaborations can be an important component of teacher education programs. Under Vásquez's supervision, undergraduate students enrolled in a research methods practicum become involved in projects investigating the literacy and language use practices available to Mexicano/Latino children in home and community contexts. As participant observers at *La Clase Mágica*, the after-school literacy program described in Chapter 6, undergraduate students assist children with their activities – computer games and telecommunication dialogues with an electronic entity known as *El Maga* – and conduct research projects on such topics as children's problem-solving strategies, language choices, and uses of literacy. Data sources for these projects include the undergraduate students' ethnographic field notes, interviews, and audio-tape recordings of children's interactions at the computer. Throughout the practicum, culture, language, and learning are key topics of student-led seminars and teleconference discussions between the undergraduate students, Vásquez, and other university students participating in similar research in

East Lansing, Michigan. During these discussions, under-graduate students share and critically examine their own and others' assumptions and generalizations about minority group members and their communities from a safe distance. Over electronic mail they openly respond to each others' comments when the topic is of a sensitive nature (e.g., such as pointing out each others' reliance on cultural stereo-types). On several occasions, students have publicly con-fronted their own narrow and unexamined perceptions about Mexicano/Latinos and their own identity and religious affiliation. For example, Lena, the 22-year-old daughter of a Mexican business man, came to terms with her own nega-tive characterization of Mexican Americans. As she worked with the children and their families, she realized that her ex-perience as a successful student in U.S. schools could not be generalized to all students of Mexican descent. For her, the realization that effort alone does not guarantee success was particularly painful. As she aptly stated, *"Mis compañeros de clase sabían más que yo, de la situación social de los méxicoameri-canos. Yo siempre he creido que era su culpa porque eran unos flojos y analfabetos."* ["My own classmates, knew better than I the social conditions of Mexican Americans. I've always thought it was their fault because they were lazy and illiterate."]

Teachers and school administrators can also learn about their students' families and communities without the help of researchers or university professors. Visiting students' homes, community centers, and community-based organi-zations and institutions may be an important first step. Like ethnographers, teachers can develop a set of interview ques-tions and or issues to discuss with parents and community members during these visits. The following list of interview topics and questions touches upon aspects of family and community life that may enhance teachers' understanding of their students.

• *Information sources in the community*
How do you find out about community events?

What community events do you participate in?

When you need information (e.g., about health care, jobs, social services), who do you go to?

- *Areas of expertise*

  What abilities and talents do you have?

  What do you enjoy doing in your spare time?

  Who do you know that brings special talents from your homeland? Describe those talents.

- *Family history*

  Tell me about your family background. Where do you come from?

  How long have you lived in the area?

  How did life in your home country differ from your life here?

- *Language use practices*

  Do you or others in your family share stories, jokes, or saying with your children? What are your children's favorite stories, jokes, or sayings?

  What kinds of things does the family talk about (e.g., around the dinner table, at bed time, at family gatherings)?

  Is someone in the family known for using language in interesting ways? Who is that person and what makes him or her special?

- *Children's everyday life at home*

  Describe a typical day in your child's life.

  How do children express themselves (i.e., their needs, feelings, humor, worries)?

  Do your children participate in activities that you feel are educational? (e.g., folk dance classes, Brownies, catechism)

- *Parents' theories about learning*

  How do children learn (i.e., to talk, read, write, do math)? What kinds of experiences help children learn? What kinds of things do you with your children that helps them learn these different things? What do others in your family do to help them learn?

What can I do as a teacher to help your child learn in the classroom?

- *Parents' views on schooling*
  How will your children benefit from school?
  What do you feel is the role of teachers in your children's education?
  What are your major concerns about the education your children are receiving?

Teachers can rely on other ways to find out about their students' lives outside of school. Teachers who are hesitant to venture into their students' communities may find it less threatening to invite parents and representatives of different community groups to share their views and experiences with faculty members during formal meetings or panel discussions. One teacher we know regularly shares an interactive journal with his students' parents. In this journal he writes about his concerns and elicits information about a variety of topics. In addition to responding to his queries, parents also voice their concerns about their children and the teacher's instruction. Teachers can also elicit the help of community members when it comes to interpreting events or phenomena that teachers don't understand or find troubling. For example, Cynthia Ballenger (1992), a preschool teacher who works with Haitian children, describes the conversations she has had with Haitian teachers, parents, and community members about the way they use language to discipline and reprimand children. Through these conversations, which have focused on verbal exchanges between adults and children that Ballenger has collected and transcribed, she has learned about the beliefs that underlie the way Haitian adults interact verbally with children and how these beliefs differ from her own. As she explains in the following excerpt from a recent article,

> I also value greatly the extent to which these conversations, by forcing me to attempt to empathize with and understand a view of the world that is in many ways very different from my

customary one, have put me in a position to reexamine values and principles that had become inaccessible under layers of assumptions."(p. 207)

Community-based research involving teachers and students can become an important part of the curriculum. For 30 years, the curriculum in Elliot Wiggington's high school English class has revolved around students' efforts to learn about the mountain community where they live (Wiggington, 1985). Initially frustrated by his students' lack of interest and engagement with a traditional grammar-oriented approach to language arts, Wiggington in the early 1960s embarked upon a period of self-reflection and experimentation that has continued unabated. Spurred by a colleague's reminder that "the beauty into which you were born is often the beauty you never see," Wiggington and his students decided to investigate the resources that surrounded them in their own community. Over the years their research, mostly captured through oral interviews and films, has focused on the knowledge, practical abilities, and aesthetic accomplishments of different community members.

INCLUSIVE STANCES TOWARD EDUCATIONAL REFORM

As many have argued most schools in this country are designed and organized to uphold the perspectives and policies of those who are in power – white, middle-class Anglos. So-called educational reforms, even those designed to better the educational plight of minority groups, tend to reflect the interests of this group as well. For example, the rationale underlying most bilingual education programs in this country emphasizes the use of children's primary language as a vehicle to transition them into an English-only curriculum rather than as a means for developing their native language as well as English.

Given the pervasiveness of this perspective, how is broad-based reform toward the perspective that we advocate to be attained? Minimally we should work toward affecting change in the attitudes of educators charged with the responsibility of teaching students. This, in part, entails making sure that teachers and administrators educate themselves about their students' communities using some of the approaches and techniques we have suggested. Another crucial step entails linking the multiple contexts and cultures that compose students' and educators' worlds so that curricular reform is a collaborative and inclusive process involving administrators, parents, teachers, students, and community members. As the Lawson experience underscores, those who participate in this kind of collaborative approach to curriculum reform would need to ensure that the interests of all participants are included in the reform process and that those of mainstream participants do not outweigh those of minority participants. Wehmiller (1992) argues that real inclusiveness within a school community comes about through the creation of a covenant which she describes in the following.

> . . . in a covenant, the members of the school community define themselves and create the definition of the school. A covenant is a promise to carry the gifts, the stories, the histories, the visions, the dreams of all the people inside of the school. It is a promise to take down the walls of exclusion. (p. 381)

Creating such a covenant entails developing a school community where the voices of parents and other community members as well as teachers and students are part of the dialogue and discussion that goes into building a schools' definition. No amount of learning about a community can replace the actual involvement of community members, including parents, in this process.

RECOGNITION PERSPECTIVES FOR ALL STUDENTS

The orientation we advocate is not restricted to minority students. All students, regardless of social class and ethnicity, benefit from an approach that acknowledges multiple backgrounds and experiences. Education that emphasizes only one set of experiences or one learning context is insufficient for preparing students to become active and informed citizens in a culturally and socially diverse society. If we want to enhance children's abilities to solve the complex problems that are part of living in a diverse society, we must acknowledge the full range of its diversity in the educational experiences that are available to all students. As we have shown in this book, ways to achieve a multiplicity of perspectives are available to minority students in and out of school. Educators must gain access to these perspectives, and find ways to help all students understand and respect one another.

Notes

1. Introduction

1. "Chicano/a" is a self-designation used by individuals who also trace their ancestry to Mexico. However, this designation identifies more closely with a life-experience in the United States. Chicanos/as often cite the historical and political struggles of Mexican origin individuals in the United States as the basis for their use of this designation. See José Limon (1981) for an analytical description of the uses the designations "Chicano, Mexicano," and "Mexican American" among the populations of South Texas.

2. "Mexicano" is a self-ascribed label used by the Mexican origin members of the community. In contrast to the term Mexican American, used by those individuals who have been in the United States one or more generations, Mexicano implies a stronger, more recent connection to Mexico.

3. In 1991, Mexican Americans constituted 7.47 percent of the undergraduate student population at the University of California at San Diego and only 4.21 percent of graduate students.

4. We make a distinction between Eastside, the Mexicano community composed of social networks and the east side, an unincorporated section of Lincoln City (see Chapter 2). The former is a construct depicting the intricate relationships of relatives, friends, and compatriots. The latter is a physical location in which Eastside is one of many communities.

197

5. These figures may be conservative. Browning and Cullen (1986) concluded that the 1980 census omitted approximately 2.5 million undocumented immigrants from Mexico.

6. According to *California Tomorrow,* children who enter school not speaking English may or may not be foreign born. For a variety of reasons, some of which are articulated in the various chapters of this book, "approximately 10–25 percent of Spanish monolingual children are U.S. born (p. 14)."

2. Eastside: A Mexicano Community

1. The names of participants in the three studies have been changed; place names that might identify participants also have been changed.

2. After San Jose and San Francisco, the east side of Lincoln City has the largest concentration of Mexicano immigrants in the Bay Area.

3. Mrs. Nuñez's remarks were audio-taped by Shannon on September 20, 1986.

4. Occasionally, Mexicanos in the area referred to the east side as "Little Casitas" because of a common belief that the Mexicano population came from the town of Las Casitas in Michoacán. Despite the number of residents from Las Casitas, Mexicanos from other regions of Mexico such as Jalisco, Zacatecas, and Mexico City have also settled there.

5. The comments were made by Mrs. Orozco to Vásquez, June 7, 1987.

6. Authors like Camarillo (1979) argue that these physical boundaries are an important defining feature of a barrio.

7. The speaker, Mrs. Ramirez, is a native of Zacatecas who came to the east side over 25 years ago. Her remarks were collected by Pease-Alvarez on June 10, 1991.

8. The school registration forms used at Morehead Elementary School during the time of Shannon's study indicate the employment status of parents.

9. Sal participated in Shannon's study.

10. Mrs. Neruda and Mrs. Cristobal were participants in Vásquez's study.

11. Medicinal plants, such as rue, mint, and marijuana are found in many of the gardens, as well as patches of corn or squash. Many of the regional foods prepared at home – *chepos* [corn

husk dish], *morisquete* [boiled rice and beans], *menudo de chivo* [goat tripe dish] – are rarely available in the restaurants of Michoacán.

12. *La sobadora* and *la señora* are knowledge sources in Vásquez's study.

13. Members of the Mexicano community of Eastside were not always in agreement as to the proper response to IRCA. Some refused to answer the call to apply for amnesty, citing that *"ese barullo se va apasiguar con tiempo,"* ["all that noise will settle down after a while"] and things would go back to being the same for the undocumented. Some feared that they would be denied amnesty and the U.S. government would subsequently deport them. Many returned to Mexico fearing that their safety and employment were compromised by the new law.

14. The Orozco family in Vásquez's study made numerous visits to their doctor in Tijuana, Mexico.

15. Mrs. Zapata shared her concerns when Vásquez collected data for her study.

16. The term "Hispanic" is the official title given by governmental agencies to individuals whose surname is Spanish or who are identified as Spanish-speaking. This category encompasses Mexican Americans, Mexican immigrants, and any number of Latin and Central American groups.

17. As part of her research in progress on language shifts in the east side, Pease-Alvarez has interviewed Mexicano/Latino parents who want their children's teachers to use more English in their classrooms.

3. Home and School Contexts for Language Learning

1. In their later work, Scollon and Scollon (1981) concluded that vertical constructions were not essential to a child's syntactic development in English. In support of this claim, they provide the following explanation.

    Bloom (1973) had observed the same phenomenon but had felt that these early constructions were not syntactic. At the same time the work of Peters (1977, 1978) had convinced us that children with very different learning strategies were achieving essentially the same structural goals.

Nelson (1975) had pointed out important differences in referentiality among children and further pointed out that what appeared to be significant was the matching between child and caregivers on strategies (p. 92).

2. Pease-Alvarez (1991) noted use of contingent queries among older children at an Eastside elementary school that is moving toward a whole language approach to learning.

3. We cannot comment on the role Arturo, Néstor's father, had on his development. He did not want to be tape recorded.

4. This appears to be based on a newscast about a bombing that Néstor overheard on the radio.

5. This study investigates native language maintenance and shift to English among 64 Mexican descent children and their families. All participants in the study are members of the Eastside community (Pease-Alvarez, 1993).

4. Bilingual Children Crossing Cultural Borders

1. Of Shannon's five subjects, Sal and Leti were the most proficient in English and Spanish at the time of the study. Eventually the other children, two of whom were recent arrivals to the United States, also attained high levels of English as well as Spanish proficiency.

2. Mrs. Larson was the favorite teacher of many Eastside children. With more than 20 years of experience in the school district, she was completely dedicated to her students. She spent time with students both in school and out. She kept her classroom open after school for anyone interested in doing homework, reading, using the computer, playing with and taking care of the guinea pigs, and/or eating – she kept a supply of leftovers from the cafeteria in her classroom, as well as instant soups and canned foods. Children of all ages spent their after-school time in Mrs. Larson's classroom. She regularly took children camping, hiking, fishing, and biking on weekends and over the summer, and invited children to her home, on the west side of Lincoln City, where she lived alone.

3. Mrs. Macías may have chosen not to intervene here because she understood much of what the doctor and her daughter were saying and because she knew that Shannon was in the

waiting room and could be called upon to conclude this office visit to her satisfaction.

4. See, for example, the classic study by Leopold, 1949.

5. Negotiating Culture and Language in the Home

1. The IRCA law required that those individuals who applied for amnesty take 40 hours instruction in English. There was no set curriculum, although social studies was the content area that most classes drew on for instruction. Enforcement of this requirement was rather weak. To meet the requirement, grantees had to show proof of having attended a course by providing a course certificate.

2. Despite the socioeconomic differences distinguishing Mr. Zapata from the other adults in the study, the cultural and linguistic patterns salient in his family's interactions were indistinct from the other three families. Spanish was the primary language of his U.S. born children, and the family was active in many relations of exchange among members of Eastside's Mexicano community.

3. Thus, nearly all the collected data are in Spanish.

4. The notion of text in this chapter extends beyond the conventional written form. Text, in this case, refers to the meanings and nuances of information or knowledge that is embodied in any number of contexts such as speech, print, and symbols or images in photographs, pictures or drawings. Thus, a text can be a traffic sign, a poster on a wall, a joke, as well as a story from a book.

5. The Neruda family, for example, made 400-mile trips to a doctor on the Mexican side of the border after they lost "faith" in the American medical system.

6. According to *Sprouses Income Tax Handbook*, "trying to follow the tax law regarding nonresidents is like trying to follow a set of foot prints that double back and trample all over each other. Even a magnifying glass isn't much help" (p. 527).

6. Moving Toward a Recognition Perspective

1. The teacher participating in this exchange spent considerable time reflecting on and revising her approach to discussion

with students. Eventually, she succeeded in engaging her students in open-ended discussions about the books that they read. See Bird and Alvarez (1987) for a description of this approach.

2. The Fifth Dimension evolved from an in-site, after-school educational activity targeting children identified as being at severe risk of academic failure (Cole and Nicolopoulou, 1991). Sites were also created in a black and a Latino neighborhood, directed by LCHC members Alonzo Anderson and Esteban Díaz, and Luis Moll, respectively. At *La Clase Mágica*, minority children became again the target population of LCHC's efforts; as they had been in the early eighties.

3. *El Maga* is an electronic entity who supervises the activities at *La Clase Mágica*. As the only true authority in the system, the children write to him/her to recount their progress through the maze or to ask for guidance in solving the problems of the games. Another function of *El Maga* is to prompt children to continue on their path in the maze and to attend to the cultural and linguistic aspects embedded in their environment. For example, on one occasion, *El Maga* asked a correspondent what *Malinche*, the name of one of the rooms, meant. The child inquired of the adults around her, inspiring an extended discussion about this Mexican historical figure.

4. Several of the bilingual/monolingual programs were created by the Bilingual Instructional Technology (BIT), a federally funded Title VII project, at San Diego University in courses taught by Bernie Dodge, Associate Professor of Educational Technology. The abject lack of educational software in Spanish is a resource constraint in providing equal access to both languages.

5. There were, for example, significant differences between the resources available to children in East Lansing, Michigan, and those available to children in Solana Beach, California. The former is *La Clase Mágica*'s counterpart in the Midwest. Together both sites make up the Bilingual Partnership of the Distributed Literacy Consortium, an Andrew Mellon Research Collective.

References

Achor, S. and Morales, A. 1990. Chicanas holding doctoral degrees: Social reproduction and cultural ecological perspectives. *Anthropology and Education Quarterly.* 21(3):269–87.

Anderson, A. B. and Stokes, S. J. 1984. Social and institutional influences on the development and practice of literacy. In H. Goelman, A. Oberg, and F. Smith (eds.), *Awakening to Literacy,* 24–37. Portsmouth, NH: Heinemann Educational Books.

Anzaldúa, G. C. (1987). *Borderlands/La Frontera: The New Mestiza.* San Francisco, CA: Spinsters/Aunt Lute.

Arora, S. L. (1972). Proverbial Exaggerations in English and Spanish. *Proverbium.* 18:675–83.

Au, K. H. 1980. Participation structures in a reading lesson with Hawaiian children: Analysis of a culturally appropriate instructional event. *Anthropology and Education Quarterly.* 11(2):91–115.

Au, K. and Jordan, K. 1981. Teaching reading to Hawaiian children: finding a culturally appropriate solution. In H. Trueba, G. P. Guthrie, and K. Au (eds.), *Culture in the Bilingual Classroom: Studies in Classroom Ethnography,* 139–62, Rowley, MA: Newberry House.

Au, K. H. and Mason, J. 1986. *Reading Instruction for Today.* Glenview, IL: Scott, Foresman.

Ballenger, C. 1992. Because you like us: The language of control. *Harvard Educational Review.* 62(2):199–208.

Bialystok, E. 1986. Factors in the growth of linguistic awareness. *Child Development.* 57:498–510.

References

Bialystok, E., and Ryan, E. B. 1985. Toward a Definition of Meta-linguistic Skill. *Merrill-Palmer Quarterly.* 31(3):229–51.

Bird, L. B. and Alvarez, L. P. 1987. Beyond comprehension: The power of literature study for language minority students. *Elementary ESOL Education News.* 10(1):1–3.

Bloom, L. 1970. *Language Development: Form and Function in Emerging Grammars.* Cambridge, MA: MIT Press.

Boggs, S. 1985. *Speaking, Relating, and Learning: A Study of Hawaiian Children at Home and at School.* Norwood, NJ: Ablex.

Bourdieu, P. and Passeron, J. C. 1990. *Reproduction in Education, Society, and Culture.* 2nd ed. R. Nice, trans. London: Sage.

Bowles, S. and Gintis, H. 1976. *Schooling in Capitalist America.* New York: Basic Books.

Brown, R. 1968. The development of Wh-questions in child speech. *Journal of Verbal Learning and Verbal Behavior.* 7:279–90.

Brown, R. and Bellugi, U. 1964. Three processes in the acquisition of syntax. *Harvard Education Review.* 34:133–51.

Browning, H. L. and Cullen, R. M. 1986. The complex demographic formation of the U.S. Mexican Origin population, 1970–1980. In H. L. Browning and R. O. de la Garza (eds.), *Mexican Immigrants and Mexican Americans: An Evolving Relationship.* 37–54. University of Texas at Austin: Center for Mexican American Studies.

Bureau of the Census. June, 1991. *1990 Census Profile: Race and Hispanic Origin.* U.S. Department of Commerce.

California Tomorrow. 1988. *Immigrant Students and the California Public Schools: Crossing the Schoolhouse Border.* California Tomorrow Policy Research Report. San Francisco, CA: California Tomorrow Immigrant Students Project.

Calkins, L. M. 1986. *The Art of Teaching Writing.* Portsmouth, NH: Heinemann.

Camarillo, A. 1979. *Chicanos in a Changing Society: From Mexican Pueblos to American Barrios in Santa Barbara and Southern California, 1848–1930.* Cambridge: Harvard University Press.

Campbell, R. N. and Lindholm, K. J. 1987. *Conservation of Language Resources.* University of California at Los Angeles: Center for Language Education and Research.

Cazden, C. 1979. Peekaboo as an instructional model: Discourse development at home and school. *Papers and Reports on Child Language Development.* 17:1–19.

References

Chavez, L. 1991. *Out of the Barrio: Toward New Politics of Hispanic Assimilation*. New York: Basic Books.

Cintron, R. 1991. Reading and writing graffiti: A reading. *The Quarterly Newsletter of the Laboratory of Comparative Human Cognition*. 13(1):21–5.

Clark, M. M. 1984. Literacy at home and at school: Insights from a study of young fluent readers. In H. Goelman, A. Oberg, and F. Smith (eds.), *Awakening to Literacy*, 122–30. Portsmouth, NH: Heinemann Educational Books.

Cole, M. 1990. Capitalizing on diversity: A proposal for a distributed literacy consortium. Andrew Mellon Foundation Research Proposal UCSD 92-5215. La Jolla, CA: Laboratory of Comparative Human Cognition.

Cole, M. and Bruner, J. S. 1971. Cultural differences and inferences about psychological process. *American Psychologist*, 26(10):867–76.

Cole, M. and Nicolopoulou, A. 1991. Creating sustainable new forms of educational activity in after-school settings. La Jolla, CA: A Final Report to the Spencer Foundation.

Commins, N. L. 1991. Dilemmas of bilingual teachers: Planning for instruction in two languages. Paper presented at the meeting of the American Anthropological Association, November, 1991. Chicago, IL.

Crawford, J. 1989. *Bilingual Education: History, Politics, Theory and Practice*. Trenton, NJ: Crane.

Cummins, J. 1981. The role of primary language development in promoting educational success for language minority students. In California State Department of Education, Office of Bilingual Education, (ed.), *Schooling and Language Minority Children*, 3–49. Los Angeles: California State University, Evaluation, Dissemination and Assessment Center.

Cummins, J. 1989. *Empowering Minority Students*. Sacramento: California Association for Bilingual Education.

deLeon, L. 1990. "Can you use Spanish words to spell the words?" Authority and metalanguage in court. Paper presented at a meeting of the Laboratory of Comparative Human Cognition, November 9, 1990. San Diego, CA.

Delgado-Gaitan, C. 1990. *Literacy for Empowerment: The Role of Parents in Children's Education*. New York: Falmer Press.

Edwards, P. A. 1987. Working with families from diverse backgrounds. In D. S. Strickland and E. J. Cooper (eds.), *Educating*

References

Black Children: America's Challenge. 92–104. Washington D.C.: Howard University, Bureau of Educational Research, School of Education.

Elías-Olivares, L. 1977. *Ways of Speaking in a Chicano Community: A Sociolinguistic Approach.* Ph.D. diss. University of Texas at Austin, 1976. Ann Arbor, MI: Xerox University Microfilms.

Elías-Olivares, L., Leone, E. A., Cisneros, R., and Gutiérrez, J. (eds.) 1985. *Spanish Language Use and Public Life in the United States.* New York: Mouton.

Erickson, F. 1987. Transformation and school success: The politics and culture of educational achievement. *Anthropology and Education Quarterly.* 18:335–56.

Erickson, F. and Mohatt, G. 1982. Cultural organization of participation structures in two classrooms of Indian students. In G. Spindler (ed.), *Doing the Ethnography of Schooling: Educational Anthropology in Action.* New York: Holt, Rinehart, and Winston.

Flores, B. M. 1982. Language interference or influence: Toward a theory for Hispanic bilingualism. Ph.D. diss., The University of Arizona, Tucson.

Foley, D. E. 1990. *Learning Capitalist Culture: Deep in the Heart of Texas.* Philadelphia: University of Pennsylvania Press.

1991. Reconsidering anthropological explanations of ethnic school failure. *Anthropology and Education Quarterly.* 22(1): 121–39.

Fonseca, O. and Moreno, L. 1984. *Jaripo, Pueblo de Migrantes.* Lázaro Cárdenas, A. C.: Centro de Estudios de la Revolución Mexicana.

Freire, P., and Macedo, D. 1987. *Literacy: Reading the Word and the World.* Cambridge: Bergin & Garvey.

Galarza, E. 1971. *Barrio Boy.* Notre Dame, IA: University of Notre Dame Press.

Gibson, M. A. 1987. The school performance of immigrant minorities: A comparative view. *Anthropology and Education Quarterly.* 18(4):262–75.

Goodlad, J. 1984. *A Place Called School.* New York: McGraw Hill.

Grosjean, F. 1982. *Life With Two Languages.* Cambridge: Harvard University Press.

Guerra, J. (1991). The acquisition and use of literacy skills and literate behaviors in families of Mexican origin. Ph.D. diss., University of Illinois, Chicago.

Harris, Brian. 1977. The importance of natural translation. *Working Papers on Bilingualism*, 12:96–114.

Harris, B. and Sherwood, G. 1978. Translating as an innate skill. In D. Gerver & H. W. Sinaiko (eds.), *Language Interpretation and Communication*, 155–70. New York: Plenum Press.

Heath, S. B. 1980. What no bedtime story means: Narrative skills at home and at school. *Language in Society* 11(2):49–76.

1982. Questioning at home and at school: A comparative study. In G. Spindler, (ed.), *Doing the Ethnography of Schooling: Educational Anthropology in Action*. New York: Holt, Rinehart, and Winston.

1983. *Ways with Words: Language, Life and Work in Communities and Classrooms*. Cambridge University Press.

1984. Linguistics and education. *Annual Review of Anthropology.* 13:251–74.

1986. Sociocultural contexts of language development. In California State Department of Education (ed.), *Beyond Language: Social and cultural factors in schooling and language minority students.* 143–86. Los Angeles: California State University, Evaluation, Dissemination and Assessment Center.

Heath, S. B. and Hoffman, D. M. 1986. Interactive reading and writing in elementary classrooms (guidebook for film, *Inside Learners*). Available from S. B. Heath, Stanford University.

Heath, S. B. and Thomas, C. 1984. The achievement of preschool literacy for mother and child. In H. Goelman, A. Oberg, and F. Smith (eds.), *Awakening to Literacy*, 51–72. Portsmouth, NH: Heinemann.

Hernández-Chávez, E. and Curtis, J. K. 1984. "The graphic sense hypothesis or You can't read firecrackers." In C. Rivera (ed.), *Placement Procedures in Bilingual Education: Education and Policy Issues.* Clevedon Avon, England: Multilingual Matters Ltd.

Hornberger, N. H. 1989. The continua of biliteracy. *Review of Educational Research.* 59(3):271–96.

Hymes, D. 1972. Models of the interaction of language and social life. In J. J. Gumperz and D. Hymes (eds.), *Directions in Sociolinguistics: The ethnography of communication*, 25–71. New York: Holt, Rinehart, and Winston.

John, V. P. 1972. Styles of learning – styles of teaching: Reflections on the education of Navajo children. In C. B. Cazden, V. P. John, and D. Hymes (eds.), *Functions of Language in the Classroom*, 331–43. New York: Teachers College Press.

References

Jordan, C. 1977. *Maternal Teaching, Peer Teaching, and School Adaptation in Urban Hawaiian Populations*. Honolulu: The Kamehameha Early Education Program.

1984. Cultural compatibility in the education of ethnic minority children: Implications for mainland educators. *Educational Research Quarterly*, 8(4):59–71.

Jordan, C. and Tharp, R. (1984). Level of analysis and the specification of sources of academic underachievement for minority cultural groups: Evidence from the Hawaiian case. Revised version of a paper presented at the Annual Meeting of the American Anthropological Association, November 1983. Honolulu: Kamehameha Schools, Center for Development of Early Education.

Kalantzis, M., Cope, B., Noble, G. and Poynting, S. 1990. *Cultures of Schooling: Pedagogies for Cultural Difference and Social Access*. London: The Falmer Press.

Keefe, S. E. and Padilla, A. M. 1987. *Chicano Ethnicity*. Albuquerque: University of New Mexico Press.

Krashen, S. D. and Biber, D. 1989. *On Course: Bilingual Education's Success in California*. Sacramento: California Association for Bilingual Education.

Langer, J. A. (1987). A Sociocognitive perspective on literacy. In J. A. Langer (ed.), *Language, Literacy, and Culture: Issues of Society and Schooling*, 1–38. Norwood, NJ: Ablex.

Laosa, L. 1977. Socialization, education, and continuity: The importance of the sociocultural context. *Young Children*. 32(5):21–6.

Leichter, H. J. 1984. Families as environments for literacy. In H. Goelman, A. Oberg, and F. Smith (eds.), *Awakening to Literacy*, 38–50. Portsmouth, NH: Heinemann Educational Books.

Leopold, W. F. 1949. *Speech Development of a Bilingual Child: A Linguist's Record. Vol. 4. Diary from Age 2*. Evanston, IL: Northwestern University Press.

Limón, J. 1981. The folk performance of "Chicano" and the cultural limits of political ideology. In R. Bauman and R. D. Abrams (eds.), *And Other Neighborly Names: Social Process and Cultural Image in Texas Folklore*, 197–225. Austin: The University of Texas Press.

1986. Language, Mexican immigration, and the "human connection": A perspective from the ethnography of communication.

In H. Browning and R. O. de la Garza (eds.), *Mexican Immigrants and Mexican-Americans: An Evolving Relationship*, 194–210. Austin: The University of Texas Center for Mexican-American Studies.

In Press. The greater Mexican Corrido and Americo Paredes as poet: On tradition, poetic influence and cultural history. In L. Brown Ruoff (ed.), *The New American Literary History*. New York: Modern Language Association.

Long, M. 1983. Native speaker/non-native speaker conversation and the negotiation of comprehensible input. *Applied Linguistics*. 4(2):126–141.

Maldonado-Guzman, A. A. 1980. Theoretical and methodological issues in ethnographic study of teachers' differential treatment of children in bilingual classrooms. In M. Saravia-Shore and S. F. Arvizu (eds.), *Cross-Cultural Literacy: Ethnographies of Communication in Multiethnic Classrooms*. New York: Garland Publishing.

Malakoff, M. 1991. Natural translation ability in French-English bilingual school-age children: A study of source language errors in naive child translators. Ph.D. diss., Yale University.

Malakoff, M. and Hakuta, K. 1991. Translation skill and metalinguistic awareness in bilinguals. In E. Bialystok (ed.), *Language Processing in Bilingual Children*, 141–67. Cambridge University Press.

McCarthy, K. F. and Valdez Burciaga, R. 1985. *Current and Future Effects of Mexican Immigration in California: Executive Summary*. Santa Monica, CA: The Rand Corporation.

McDowell, J. H. 1982. Sociolinguistic contours in the verbal art of Chicano children. *Aztlan–International Journal of Chicano Studies Research*. 13(1–2):165–93.

McGroarty, M. 1992. The societal context of bilingual education. *Educational Researcher*. 21(2):7–9.

Mehan, H. 1979. *Learning Lessons: The Social Organization of Classroom Behavior*. Cambridge: Harvard University Press.

1991. *Sociological Foundations Supporting the Study of Cultural Diversity*. Research No. R117G10022. National Center for Research on Cultural Diversity and Second Language Learning. Research Report: Office of Educational Research and Improvement of the U.S. Department of Education.

1992. Understanding inequality in schools. *The Sociology of Education*. 65(1):1–20.

References

Michaels, S. 1981. "Sharing time": Children's narrative styles and differential access to literacy. *Language in Society* 10(3): 423–42.

Michaels, S. and Collins, J. 1984. Oral discourse styles: Classroom interaction and the acquisition of literacy. In D. Tannen (ed.), *Coherence in Spoken and Written Discourse*, 219–44. Norwood, NJ: Ablex.

Miller, P. J. 1982. *Amy, Wendy, and Beth: Language Learning in South Baltimore.* Austin: University of Texas Press.

Moll, L. C. 1992. Bilingual classroom studies and community analysis: Some recent trends. *Educational Researcher: Special Issue on Bilingual Education.* 21(2):20–4.

Moll, L. C., Amanti, C., Neff, D., Gonzalez, N. 1992. Funds of knowledge for teaching: Using a qualitative approach to connect homes and classrooms. *Theory into Practice.* 31(2):132–41.

Moll, L. C. and Diaz, S. 1987. Change as the goal of educational research. *Anthropology and Education Quarterly.* 18:300–11.

Ninio, A. and Bruner, J. S. 1977. The achievement and antecedents of labeling. *Journal of Child Language,* 5:1–15.

Ochs, E. 1988. *Culture and language development.* Cambridge University Press.

Ogbu, J. U. 1978. *Minority Education and Caste: The American System in Cross-Cultural Perspective.* New York: Academic Press.

  1982. Cultural discontinuities and schooling. *Anthropology and Education Quarterly.* 13(4):290–307.

  1987. Variability in minority school performance: A problem in search of an explanation. *Anthropology and Education Quarterly.* 18(4):312–34.

Ogbu, J. U. and Matute-Bianchi, M. E. 1986. Understanding sociocultural factors: Knowledge, identity, and school adjustment. In *Beyond Language: Social and Cultural Factors in Schooling Language Minority Students,* 73–142. Los Angeles: Evaluation, Dissemination, and Assessment Center, California State University.

Parades, A. 1958. *With a Pistol in His Hand.* Austin: Texas University Press.

  1984. On ethnographic work among minority groups: A folklorist perspective. In R. Romo and R. Paredes (eds.), *New Directions in Chicano Scholarship,* 1–32. Santa Barbara: Center for Chicano Studies, University of California.

References

Pease-Alvarez, L. 1989. Case Studies; United States (California). Working Document. Education and Cultural and Linguistic Pluralism: Innovative Schools. Organization for Economic Co-operation and Development.

___. 1991. Oral contexts for literacy development in a Mexican immigrant community. *The Quarterly Newsletter of the Laboratory of Comparative Human Cognition.* 13(1):9–13.

___. 1993. Moving in and out of bilingualism: Investigating native language maintenance and shift in Mexican descent children. Research Report Six. National Center for Research on Cultural Diversity and Second Language Learning. Office of Educational Research and Improvement of the U.S. Department of Education.

Pease-Alvarez, L. and Hakuta, K. 1992. Enriching our views of bilingualism and bilingual education. *Educational Researcher.* 21(2):4–6.

Peninsula Times Tribune 1991. Wealth, Poverty, and the Sequoia Gap. May 12, B.6.

Peñalosa, F. 1978. Sociolinguistics and the Chicano community. In Z. A. Kruszewski, R. L. Hough, and J. Ornstein Garcia, (eds.), *Politics and Society in the Southwest: Ethnicity and Chicano Pluralism*, 225–46. Boulder, CO: Westview Press.

___. 1980. *Chicano Sociolinguistics: A Brief Introduction.* Rowley, MA: Newbury House.

Philips, S. U. 1983. *The Invisible Culture: Communication in Classroom and Community on the Warm Springs Indian Reservation.* New York: Longman.

Piestrup, A. 1973. *Black Dialect Interference and Accommodation of Reading Instruction in First Grade.* Berkeley: Monographs of the Language Behavior Research Laboratory.

Porter, R. P. 1990. *Forked Tongue: The Politics of Bilingual Education.* New York: Basic Books.

Puckett, J. L. 1989. *Foxfire Reconsidered.* Urbana, IL: University of Illinois Press.

Ramírez, D. J. 1991. *Final Report: Longitudinal Study of Structured English Immersion Strategy, Early-Exit and Late-Exit Transitional Bilingual Education Programs for Language Minority Children.* Washington, D.C.: Office of Bilingual Education.

Ratner, N. and Bruner, J. S. 1977. Games, social exchange and the acquisition of language. *Journal of Child Language.* 5:391–401.

References

Rosaldo, R. 1985. *Assimilation Revisited*. Working Paper Series No. 9. Palo Alto, CA: Stanford University, Stanford Center for Chicano Research.

Salinas, Raúl. 1972. "A trip through the mind jail." In Antonio Castañeda Schular, Tomas Ybarra Frausto, and Joseph Sommers (eds.), *Literatura Chicana: Texto y contexto*, 182–6. Englewood Cliffs, NJ: Prentice Hall.

Sánchez, R. 1983. *Chicano Discourse*. Rowley, MA: Newbury House.

Schacter, J. 1986. Three approaches to the study of input. *Language Learning*. 36:211–25.

Schieffelin, B. B. and Cochran-Smith, M. 1984. Learning to read culturally: Literacy before schooling. In H. Goelman, A. Oberg, and F. Smith (eds.), *Awakening to Literacy*, 3–23. Portsmouth, NH: Heinemann.

Schieffelin, B. B. and Ochs, E. 1986. Language socialization. *The Annual Review of Anthropology*. 15:163–91.

Schumann, J. H. 1978. The acculturation model for second-language acquisition. *Journal of Multilingual and Multicultural Development*. 7:379–92.

Scribner, S. and Cole, M. 1981. *The Psychology of Literacy*. Cambridge, MA: Harvard University Press.

Scollon, R. 1979. A real early stage. An unzipped condensation of a dissertation on child language. In E. Ochs and B. B. Schieffelin (eds.), *Developmental Pragmatics*, 215–28. New York: Academic Press.

Scollon, R. and Scollon, S. 1981. *Narrative, Literacy, and Face in Interethnic Communication*. Norwood, NJ: Ablex.

Shannon, S. M. 1987. English in el Barrio: A sociolinguistic study of second language contact. Ph.D. diss. Stanford University.

  1989. An ethnography of a fourth-grade bilingual classroom: Patterns of English and Spanish. In D. J. Bixler-Márquez, G. K. Green, and J. L. Ornstein-Galicia (eds.), *Mexican-American Spanish in its Societal and Cultural Contexts* (Rio Grande Series in Language and Linguistics, No. 3), 35–50. Brownsville, TX: Pan American University.

Snow, C. E. 1977. Mothers'-speech research: From input to interaction. In C. E. Snow and C. A. Ferguson (eds.), *Talking to Children*, 31–49. Cambridge University Press.

  1983. Literacy and language: Relationships during the preschool years. *Harvard Educational Review*, 53(2):165–189.

Snow, C. E. and Dickinson, D. K. 1992. Skills that aren't basic in the new conception of literacy. Unpublished manuscript.

Suárez-Orozco, M. 1987. Toward a psychosocial understanding of Hispanic adaptation to American schooling. In H. T. Trueba (ed.), *Success or Failure? Learning and the Language Minority Student*, 156–68. Cambridge, MA: Newbury House.

Taylor, D. 1981. The family and the development of literacy skills and values. *Journal of Research in Reading* 4(2):92–103.

Tharp, R. and Gallimore, R. 1988. *Rousing Minds to Life: Teaching, Learning, and Schooling in Social Context*. Cambridge University Press.

1989. Rousing schools to life. *American Educator.* 13(2):20–5, 46–52.

1991. *The Instructional Conversation: Teaching and learning in Social Activity.* The National Center for Research on Cultural Diversity and Second Language Learning, University of California.

Thiery, Christopher. 1978. True bilingualism and second-language learning. In D. Gerver and H. Wallace Sinaiko (eds.), *Language Interpretation and Communication*, 145–54. New York: Plenum Press.

Vásquez, O. A. 1989. Connecting oral language strategies to literacy: An ethnographic study among four Mexican immigrant families. Ph.D. diss. Stanford University, Stanford, CA.

1992. A Mexicano perspective: Reading the world in a multicultural setting. In D. E. Murray (ed.), *Diversity as Resource: Redefining Cultural Literacy.* Alexandria, VA: Teachers of English to Speakers of Other Languages, Inc.

Vélez-Ibañez, C. G. and Greenberg, J. B. 1992. Formation and transformation of funds of knowledge among U.S. Mexican households. *Anthropology and Education Quarterly.* 23(4):313–35.

Veltman, C. 1988. *The Future of the Spanish in the United States.* New York and Washington, D.C.: Hispanic Policy Development Project.

Vogt, L. A., Jordan, C., and Tharp, R. 1987. Explaining school failure, producing school success: Two cases. *Anthropology and Education Quarterly.* 18(4):276–86.

Wehmiller, P. L. 1992. When the walls come tumbling down. *Harvard Educational Review.* 62(3):373–83.

West, C. 1984. *Routine Complications: Troubles with Talk between Doctors and Patients.* Bloomington, IA: Indiana University Press.

References

Wiggington, E. 1985. *Sometimes a Shining Moment: The Foxfire Experience.* Garden City, NY: Anchor Books.

Willis, P. 1977. *Learning to Labour.* Lexington, MA: D. C. Heath.

Wong-Fillmore, L. 1991. When learning a second language means losing the first. *Early Childhood Research Quarterly.* 6(3):323–46.

Ybarra-Frausto, T. 1984. I can still hear the applause. La farándula Chicana: Carpas y tandas de variedad. In N. Kanelos, (ed.), *Hispanic Theatre in the United States.* Houston, TX: Arte Público Press.

Zentella, A. C. 1980. Hablamos los dos: We Speak Both: Growing up bilingual in El Barrio. Ph.D. diss. University of Pennsylvania.

Index

analytic strategies, 17, 126, 132
  development of, 138
  and literacy, 113–14, 151
  in oral and written texts, 116

barrio, 23–5, 81
bilingual education, 150, 169,
  171, 194
  and bilingualism, 109, 148,
  in Eastside, 40–4, 84
  in Northern California, 169–77
  (*see also* Spanish Immersion
  Program)

Chicano/a, 2, 3, 7, 15, 85, 197n1
computers. *See also* La Clase Mágica
  use of with reading and writing, 152
contingent queries, 56–73, 78–9
  as clarification and elaboration
  requests, 5, 46, 56–60, 68,
  72, 89
  at home, 62–7
  and literacy development, 59,
  60, 158
  older children's use of, 200n2
  as reading and writing
  support, 60
  at school, 61–2; 67–73
  as vertical constructions, 59

cross-cultural interactions, 79.
  See also intercultural trans-
  action(s); interethnic communication; interethnic
  encounters
cultural and linguistic
  repertoire, 29
cultural and linguistic resources.
  See resources
cultural brokers, children as, 13,
  37, 81, 185
cultural capital, 11
cultural conflict in classrooms, 149
cultural convergence, 47, 79
curriculum, 18. *See also* instruction
  culturally responsive, 9, 168–9,
  179
  at La Escuelita, 53–4
  making relevant, 188

deficit hypothesis, 8, 40

Eastside, 1, 14, 22, 24
  as distinct from the east side of
  Lincoln City, 20–1, 197n3
  housing and employment issues
  in, 26–8
  language patterns in, 29–38,
  83–5, 112–13, 119
  Mexican migration to, 21–2

215

knowledge
  access to, 136, 141
  activity as a source of, 29
  linguistic and cultural, 108
  Mexicano children and, 12, 92–3
  multiple sources of, 18, 89, 91–3
  outside of Mexican home, 33–6
  social interactions demands of, 12
  social networks and, 34–6, 189
  socioreligious cultural, 36
    uses of, 16, 29–30, 95, 112
    in problem-solving discussions, 17, 127 (see also Reconstructions)

La Clase Mágica, 159–69, 190. See also The Fifth Dimension
  children's choice of language in, 163–8
  computers in, 160
  cultural and linguistic resources in, 161, 168
  knowledge sources in, 163
  literacy in, 160–1, 167
language acquisition. See also language development; language learning; language socialization
  clarifications and elaborations in, 89
  and comprehensible input, 163
  scaffolding and, 89
language broker, 96, 105, 127. See also translator
language development, 51, 66. See also language acquisition; language learning; language socialization
  adult questioning strategies and, 56–72
  conversation in, 73, 90
  Eastside's parents' perspectives on, 66, 74
  of ethnic minority children, 47

  and literacy development, 45
  in middle-class, English-speaking homes, 46–7, 61
  and social context, 7
  and social networks, 95
  teachers and, 73
  vertical constructions in, 199n1
language learning, 56. See also language acquisition; language learning; language socialization
  of ethnic minority children, 47
  as a negotiated activity, 46
  parents' role in, 76
  sociocultural contexts for, 21
language socialization, 1, 17, 51, 61, 67, 73, 79, 90, 159. See also language acquisition; language development; language learning
  adult role in, 17, 46, 51, 73–6, 142
  child rearing practices and, 61, 66
  child's role in, 51, 73–4, 142, 151
  cross-cultural variation of, 5–8, 61, 79
  scaffolding in, 6
language-use patterns, 29–31, 35, 67. See also use of language
  at home, 29–30, 52, 148
  at school, 13, 31, 52, 147
  how schooling affects, 78–9
language variation
  and cognition, 4
linguistic and cultural resources. See resources
linguistic repertoire, 30
  and cultural, 29
linguistically and culturally different children
  at school, 8, 10, 186
literacy
  conceptions of, 141
  and the cross-age tutoring project, 151–9